THE TRICKY GAME:
Deceptive Plays to Winning Bridge

by Hugh Kelsey

Published by
Devyn Press, Inc.
Louisville, Kentucky 40241

Previously published as
  THE TRICKY GAME (Max Hardy)
  and
  DECEPTIVE PLAYS (Robert Hale Ltd.)

Printed in the United States of America.

Devyn Press, Inc.
3600 Chamberlain Lane, Suite 230
Louisville, KY 40241
1-800-274-2221

ISBN 0-939460-54-8

CONTENTS

♠ ♡ ◇ ♣

INTRODUCTION

Are you regarded as a tough opponent at the bridge table, or do your friends find you easy to play against? If the latter, it is time you did something about it. You can learn to surprise your friends by cultivating a more deceptive style. This is the department of the game that offers the widest scope for improvement to average players. A small effort can reap great rewards, bringing in large numbers of dollars, master points or whatever else you play for. Progress in this field is doubly rewarding. Once you acquire even a limited reputation as a tricky opponent, the points will come rolling in not only when you are bluffing but also when your friends suspect that you are bluffing and discover, to their dismay, that you are not.

What makes for a deceptive style? Basically it is a matter of playing your cards in such a way as to conceal the strengths and weaknesses of your hand for as long as possible. By fostering illusions and creating doubts in the minds of your opponents, you try to persuade them that black is white. When offered a plausible alternative to the winning line of play or defense, your opponents, even if suspicious, will have to do some heavy guesswork. Inevitably they will sometimes guess right in spite of your best efforts. Your percentage comes from the times when they guess wrong.

There are hundreds of small ways in which illusions can be built up and we shall examine them all in this book. It is important to study deceptive plays in advance so that similar situations can be recognised when you meet them at the bridge table. The point is that there is little time to think when an opportunity presents itself. Any hesitation is likely to be fatal to the chances of success. A deceptive play is basically a confidence trick, and the con man who stammers when he tells a lie is not likely to impress his victim. Undue speed is another thing to avoid, for that is an equal giveaway. The essence of deception is smoothness. You have to maintain the same even tempo whether you are making the natural play or telling a brazen lie.

I predict that you will have a lot of fun reading this book, and even more fun when you start to put the ideas into practice. There is a special pleasure to be gained from pulling the wool over opponents' eyes and thus getting away with something that is not really on the cards. More satisfaction can be derived from a good swindle than from the most brilliant technical coup. Enjoy yourself!

Chapter 1

TRICKS WITH HONORS

One of the big advantages enjoyed by declarer in the play of the cards is that there is no need for him to pass honest information to his partner. Dummy is temporarily out of action and in no position to influence matters, so in selecting a card to play declarer can give free reign to his larcenous instincts. The idea is to sow the maximum confusion in the enemy ranks. In winning a trick declarer will often have a choice of honor cards, and the choice should not be made at random. For each combination there will be a right card and a wrong card to play, depending on what you are trying to achieve. It will sometimes be possible to induce a continuation when that is what you want and to suggest a shift when that will suit your book.

Let us start with a simple situation.

```
                    7 4 3
5 led                             Q played
                    A K 6
```

Most players know what to do when West leads a small card and East plays the queen. In a trump contract they will win with the ace, leaving open for West the possibility that his partner may have the king. Clearly if the king is used to win the first trick both defenders will know that declarer has the ace as well.

Different tactics are called for if the contract is notrumps. If declarer decides to win the first trick the card to play is the king. To win with the ace would be a giveaway, for the defenders would expect declarer to hold up if the ace were his only stopper. When you win with the king, East may receive the impression that a further lead from him will enable his partner to pick up the rest of the tricks in the suit.

6 5 2

4 led   J played

K Q 7

In the above position, when West leads a low card against your notrump contract and East plays the jack, you should again win the trick, if you decide to win it, with the king. If you win with the queen, West will know that you have the king as well and will plan his defense accordingly. When you win with the king he will be uncertain about the location of the queen. He may not be naive enough to underlead his ace once more when he regains the lead, but it is always a good thing to keep opponents in doubt about your holding.

It might be thought that if you have king and queen alone in a similar position you should win with the queen, making it plain to West that you have the king as well. But that would probably be too subtle, for West would ask himself why you were going out of your way to reveal the position. If he reached the right conclusion, on regaining the lead he would lay down his ace, felling your king, and run the rest of the suit.

So the recommended play, even when holding king-queen doubleton, is to win the first trick with the king, as declarer did on the following hand.

                        North
                        ♠ K J 10 2
                        ♡ 9 7 3
                        ◇ K 5
                        ♣ 9 7 5 4
West   *East*
♠ A 5 3   ♠ 9 7 4
♡ A J 10 6 5   ♡ 8 4 2
◇ 10 8 7 2   ◇ Q J 4 3
♣ 3   ♣ J 10 6
                        South
                        ♠ Q 8 6
                        ♡ K Q
                        ◇ A 9 6
                        ♣ A K Q 8 2

Both vulnerable.
Dealer South.

South	North
2NT	3♣
3NT	Pass

Better bidding might have led to the sounder contract of five clubs, but South played in three notrumps and West led the jack of hearts to the three, two and king. Needing to steal a ninth trick, South rejected the obvious play of a spade at trick two. First he played off the ace and king of clubs. When West discarded a diamond, South paused (quite unethically) as though digesting the news of a bad club break and then led the six of spades.

It looked to West as though declarer would need several tricks from spades, so he played low in the hope that his partner would be able to gain the lead. When the ten of spades won, of course, South made chortling noises and nine tricks.

A fair amount of space in this book is going to be devoted to countering deception, and it is not too early to make a start. Declarer would have had no chance on the above hand against defenders who used distributional signals. West would know that his partner's two of hearts indicated an odd number of cards. A singleton could be ruled out since South had denied four hearts in the bidding, thus West would be left with the certainly that East had started with three hearts and South with a doubleton. It would not be hard, in those circumstances, for West to shoot up with the ace of spades and continue with the heart ace, relying on East to unblock if he had the queen.

Distributional signals may be helpful to declarer now and then, but on balance they are of far greater value to the defense. Players using count signals have a built-in safeguard against many forms of deception.

We came to the conclusion that it would arouse suspicion to win the first trick with the queen from king-queen doubleton. That suggests the possibility of laying a trap for West when you have K Q x.

	North	
	♠ 9 4 3	
	♡ A 9 2	
	◊ Q 10 6 2	
	♣ A 8 4	
West		East
♠ A 10 8 5 2		♠ J 7
♡ Q 6 5		♡ J 10 4 3
◊ K 4		◊ 8 3
♣ 10 7 2		♣ Q J 6 5 3
	South	
	♠ K Q 6	
	♡ K 8 7	
	◊ A J 9 7 5	
	♣ K 9	

Match-point pairs.
Both vulnerable.
Dealer South.

South	North
South	*North*
1NT	3NT

West leads the five of spades and East puts in the jack. It is right to win the first trick since you have to take the diamond finesse into the West hand. You can be sure of nine tricks even if the finesse fails, but a tenth trick is always welcome at pairs. So try the effect of winning the first trick with the queen of spades instead of the more normal king. Then cross to the ace of hearts and run the ten of diamonds to the king. If West suspects your spade holding to be king-queen doubleton, he may now cash the ace of spades, presenting you with the desired overtrick.

There can be no certainty of success in situations like this. Much depends on your estimate of the defenders' abilities and their estimate of yours. The game of bluff and counter-bluff can be extended indefinitely. The important thing is to avoid becoming known as a player who always plays a certain card from a given holding. With K Q x you should win with the king most of the time, but occasionally stir the pot by winning with the queen.

7 6 2

5 led   10 played

A Q J

When you are anxious to conceal strength it is usually the higher of equal cards that is the more deceptive. In the above diagram when West leads a low card and East plays the ten, you should win with the queen, leaving the opponents in doubt about the location of the jack. If you win with the jack, West will know exactly what you have.

<pre>
          10 5 3
Q 7 6 4   J 8 2
          A K 9
</pre>

When West leads the four in this situation, avoid the lazy play of a low card from dummy. The jack will force out your king and West will know that you have a A 9 left, for with J 9 x East would have played the nine. The way to conceal your holding from West is to play the ten from the table. When this is covered by the jack and king, West will not know who has the nine and may be tempted to lead the suit again when he gets in.

<pre>
          J 10 3
K 8 7 5 4   6 2
          A Q 9
</pre>

This combination lends itself to a pretty swindle. When West leads the five against your notrump contract, the best shot is to go up with the jack as though trying to induce a cover and overtake with the queen when East plays low. If you then use an outside entry to reach dummy and take a losing finesse in another suit towards West, he is quite likely to continue his attack, expecting your ace to drop. He will be protected from such foolishness, of course, if his partner has given a count signal.

<pre>
          7 6 4
          A Q 10 9 3
</pre>

Suppose that this is your trump suit which, for want of entries to dummy, you have to tackle from your own hand. Both defenders follow with small cards when you cash the ace. Which card do you lead on the second round, the queen or the ten? Technically it's a toss-up, for there is an equal probability of finding a doubleton king or a doubleton jack. No doubt most declarers will play the queen, taking the view that it is more fun to pin a doubleton jack than to drop a doubleton king. Psychologically, too, the play of the queen on the second round has a slight advantage, for if it turns out that you have two losers in the suit only one opponent will know about it immediately. The other will be left in doubt about your holding, and this may affect his defense. Naturally if your trumps are A Q J 10 3 you should make the same second-round play of the queen instead of the lazy ten.

The advantage may seem too slender to be worth bothering about, but it is only by paying careful attention to a host of small points like this that you can hope to build up a deceptive style.

Here is a similar case:

7 5

A K J 9 8 (or A K J 10 8)

Again, if the defenders follow with low cards to the ace and king, you should continue with the jack in each case.

Playing the Known Card

When the opening lead allows your right-hand opponent to place you with a certain card, it will usually be a good idea to get rid of that card at the earliest possible moment.

8 6 4

9 5   K Q J 7 3

A 10 2

West leads the nine to his partner's jack and you decide to hold up for one round. If you play the two and then win with the ace, East will know that you have the ten left since West's lead of the nine denied that card. West will also know that you have the ten because of his partner's first-round play of the jack. It does not pay to let defenders know so much about your hand. Play the ten on the first round. When you win the second round with the ace, neither opponent can then be sure that you have a third card in the suit.

Another case:

$$K\ J\ 7\ 4$$

8   A Q 10 5 3 2

$$9\ 6$$

West leads the eight to the jack and queen. Unless you drop the nine, the card you are known to hold, East will know that it is safe for him to cash the ace.

The danger may be even more immediate.

$$10\ 7\ 4$$

Q   A J 9 8 5 3 2

$$K\ 6$$

Suppose you are playing in a trump contract and West leads the queen of a suit in which his partner has pre-empted. East puts on the ace, and you. . . . ?

If you play the six, East will certainly give his partner a ruff on the next round. Naturally you must drop the king, the card you are known to hold. Now East may shift, fearing that a continuation will set up a trick for dummy's ten. And the shift may give you a chance to dispose of your second loser on one of dummy's winners.

The position is much the same if it is West who has made the pre-emptive bid.

$$J\ 6\ 5$$

A led   7 played

$$K\ 4$$

If you play low from hand West will certainly continue the suit, knowing that it can do no harm whether his partner ruffs or produces the king. But if you casually drop the king under the ace, West may hesitate to continue for fear of establishing the jack on the table.

<pre>
            8 6 5 4
J   A 9 7 3 2
            K Q 10
</pre>

In the above case, when West leads the jack to his partner's ace, the card that East knows you to have is the queen, so get rid of it fast. If you play the ten, East will know that he can give his partner a ruff on the second round. When you drop the queen, East has to take account of the possibility that his partner has led from K J 10 or from J 10 doubleton. Instead of continuing the suit he may look for tricks elsewhere.

The middle card from three honors is often the only one that can create a problem for an opponent.

<pre>
            K 8 6 3
2 led   A played
            Q J 10
</pre>

Again you are in a trump contract, and West's lead of the two of this side suit looks ominously like a singleton. The position need not be obvious to East, however, although he does know something about your hand. East can work out that you must have the jack in the suit, and so that is the card you must drop under the ace. West would not have led the two from Q J 2 or J 10 2, but he might have from Q 10 2.

<pre>
            K 8 3 2
4 led   Q played
            J 10 9
</pre>

When you play low from dummy, East wins with the queen. This time the card you are marked with is the ten, and you must drop it under the queen to leave open for East the possibility that his partner has led from J 9 4.

                    7 6 5 3
10   A Q 8 4 2
                    K J 9

The only way to make East think twice about continuing the suit is to drop the jack, the card you are known to hold, under the ace.

                    J 8 5
A K 10 7 6   9 4 3
                    Q 2

In this case there is no question of playing a known card. Still, if you cannot afford to lose two tricks in this suit, try the effect of dropping the queen when West leads the king. The ruse may be a bit of a chestnut but it is still capable of salvaging plenty of unmakable contracts. However suspicious West may be, he cannot be sure that your queen is not a singleton, even if he and his partner are using count signals. Fortunately the card you are concealing is the two, which makes it look as though East might have started a small echo from 9 4 3 2.

The reason for dropping an honor card is not always to induce a shift. Sometimes a continuation is what you want. I am indebted to Martin Hoffman for details of the next hand, which was played by one of the great masters of deception, the late Bobby Slavenburg.

North
♠ 9 8
♡ Q 7 6
♢ 3 2
♣ K 8 7 6 5 4

West
♠ A K Q 10
♡ 10 5 4 2
♢ Q 7 6
♣ Q 2

East
♠ 5 4 3 2
♡ K J 3
♢ J 9 5 4
♣ 10 3

South
♠ J 7 6
♡ A 9 8
♢ A K 10 8
♣ A J 9

Neither vulnerable.
Dealer South.

South	West	North	East
1♣	Double	3♣	Pass
3NT	Pass	Pass	Pass

Someone seems to have stretched a little in the bidding. Certainly, if you reach dubious 22-point games like this you need to know how to handle your cards.

Slavenburg was not at all happy when West led the king of spades and dummy went down. Even if the enemy were unable to run enough spades to defeat the contract immediately, the blockage in clubs was a depressing feature. It looked as though it would be possible to run the clubs only if someone had a bare queen --a poor 12½% chance.

Slavenburg wanted better odds than that, and when West continued with a second high spade he smoothly dropped the jack. West, freed from the fear that declarer might have started with J x x x in spades, happily continued the suit. Slavenburg pitched red cards from dummy and was able to get rid of a blocking club from his hand on the last spade. When the 40% 2-2 club break materialised he had his nine tricks.

Well as declarer played on this hand, West should not have been taken in. It was reasonable to continue with a third spade when the jack appeared on the second round, but when South produced a small spade on the third round West should have taken a moment to ask himself what was going on. What can declarer be up to? He has deliberately made it easy for West to cash his spades, and the conclusion must be that for some reason he is desperate for a spade continuation.

It is not necessary to see round corners in such situations. What is good for declarer must be bad for the defense, and West should therefore have shifted to one of the red suits at trick four. With no chance to unblock the clubs, declarer would then have been defeated.

Chapter 2

FALSE IMPRESSIONS

We have seen that declarer has great freedom of action in his choice of cards and can make the play best calculated to cause confusion in the enemy ranks. It is not quite so easy for the defenders, whose urge to drop false cards has to be moderated by their need to exchange honest information with each other. It is all very well trying to fool the declarer, but the overall effect may be harmful rather than beneficial if partner is also deceived. Nevertheless, the defenders have an advantage in that *two* hands are hidden from declarer, and opportunities are plentiful.

Obligatory False Cards

There are many situations in which the defenders *must* false-card in order to offer declarer an alternative to the winning line of play. The opportunities arise when declarer is developing a long suit, often the trump suit, and when he is bound to get it right unless the defenders throw out a smoke-screen. Here are the basic positions, all of which have many variations.

```
            A J 7 3
K 5                      10 9 4
            Q 8 6 2
```

When declarer plays a low card and finesses dummy's jack, East must drop the nine or the ten. Otherwise South will be forced into the winning play of cashing the ace on the second round. The play of the nine by East creates a losing option. South may now return to hand in another suit and run the queen, hoping to pin the ten in the East hand.

```
                    3
J 10 5                                      A 4
              K Q 9 8 7 6 2
```

This is a similar case. When South plays the single-ton from dummy and wins with the king, West must drop the jack or ten to offer a choice of plays. South may now go wrong by continuing with the queen.

```
              A Q 10 7 3
K 6 2                                       9 8 5 4
              J
```

Suppose the contract is notrumps and there is only one outside entry in dummy. Needing tricks from this suit, South leads the jack, overtakes with the queen and cashes the ace. Unless East drops the eight or the nine under the ace declarer cannot go wrong on the third round.

```
              K J 8 7 3
Q 6 2                                       10 9 5
              A 4
```

Declarer starts with the ace, and if East plays the five he will continue with a finesse of the jack, picking up the entire suit. East may steal a trick for the defense if he plays the nine or ten under the ace. If declarer can afford one loser in the suit he may judge it best to go up with the king on the second round, catering for 10 9 or queen doubleton in the East hand. This ploy may bring in more than one trick for the defense if East has 10 5 and West Q 9 6 2.

```
            Q 5
J 10 3                          8 2
         A K 9 7 6 4
```

South starts with a low card to the queen and will have no trouble bringing in the suit if West plays low. But if West plays the jack or the ten a losing option appears, and South may be tempted to finesse the nine on the way back. The play is against the odds, but declarers do not always follow the odds in such situations.

```
         A 8 5 4
6                               J 9 7 2
         K Q 10 3
```

In this standard position when South starts with the king from hand, East must not fail to drop the nine to create a two-way finessing possibility. South may then go wrong by playing the queen on the second round.

If entries permit, mind you, a competent declarer will protect himself against deception in the above diagram by starting with a low card from the table. Now East can hardly afford to play the nine. For all he knows his partner may have a singleton ten, and it would be humiliating to throw away a sure defensive trick.

```
         K J 9 3
10 8 5 4                        A
         Q 7 6 2
```

This case is similar. South leads the two to dummy's jack, and the defenders have the chance of a second trick in the suit only if West plays the eight.

Single-suit diagrams look a little barren, so let's

view the next play of this type in the setting of a complete deal.

<pre>
                    North
                    ♠ A J 7 2
                    ♡ 8 5
    West   ◇ A 8 7 4   East
    ♠ 4   ♣ K 6 2   ♠ K 10 8 5
    ♡ K 10 7 3   ♡ A 9 6 2
    ◇ 10 6 5   South   ◇ J 3
    ♣ J 10 8 7 3   ♠ Q 9 6 3   ♣ 9 5 4
                    ♡ Q J 4
                    ◇ K Q 9 2
                    ♣ A Q
</pre>

Match-point pairs.

North-South vulnerable.
Dealer South.

South	North
1NT	2♣
2♠	4♠

South wins the opening club lead with the ace and plays the three of spades to dummy's jack. East should realise at this point that he will not make a second trump trick if he wins with the king, for South will play the ace on the second round and continue with the marked finesse against the ten.

The right card for East to play is the eight of spades, suggesting the possibility that he may have 10 8 doubleton. South can, of course, play safe for ten tricks by continuing with a low spade from the table, but at pairs he will be reluctant to give up the chance of eleven tricks. If East drops the eight smoothly enough, declarer may well return to hand with a club and run the queen of spades, hoping to pin the ten.

South will realise that he has been conned when

West shows out on the second round, but it will be too late to recover. He will have no way of avoiding the loss of two trumps and two heart tricks.

On the next hand declarer was lured to his doom by a neat false card.

                    North
                    ♠ Q 10 6 2
                    ♡ J 9 2
West   ◇ K 9 4   *East*
♠ K 3   ♣ A K 4   ♠ 7
♡ 7 5 3   ♡ K Q 10 8
◇ A J 8 5   *South*   ◇ Q 10 7 2
♣ 10 8 7 2   ♠ A J 9 8 5 4   ♣ J 9 3 2
                    ♡ A 6 4
                    ◇ 6 3
                    ♣ Q 6

Both vulnerable.
Dealer North.

North	*South*
1♣	1♠
2♠	4♠

West led the five of hearts and the nine was played from dummy. It seems natural for East to cover with the ten, but East realised that it could cost nothing to play the queen on the first trick, since it was his partner who had the outside entries.

South won with the ace and seized the opportunity to take a discard on the third round of clubs before playing trumps. Naturally he chose to discard a diamond rather than a heart. He feared that there might be two losers in diamonds, while he had high hopes of scoring a second heart trick with the jack.

When West came in with the king of spades he had

little option but to lead a second heart, even though he expected declarer to have the ten from the play to the first trick. However, East captured the jack of hearts with the king and cashed the ten, and the ace of diamonds scored the setting trick.

Clearly the contract would have been made if East had made the pedestrian play of the heart ten at trick one. Declarer would have discarded a heart on the third round of clubs, and would have lost one spade, one heart and one diamond.

A K 8 6 5

Q 10   7 4 3

J 9 2

With this combination South starts by leading the two from hand, and he has no chance of going wrong if West follows meekly with the ten. But if West plays the queen declarer has to take a view. He may go wrong by finessing the nine on the second round.

There is no real difference if West has the king instead of the queen.

A Q 8 6 5

K 10   7 4 3

J 9 2

If West plays the king on the first round, a losing option is created for declarer.

Q 10 3

A J 9   7 6 4

K 8 5 2

South leads the two with the obvious intention of finessing the ten. West's jack is a dead duck and he has nothing to lose by playing it immediately. This may turn out surprisingly well. After winning the queen and returning the ten to knock out the ace, South is quite likely to finesse the eight on the third round, allowing West to make a second trick in the suit after all.

The combination A J 9 lends itself particularly well to deceptive play. I am indebted to Swedish International Anders Wahlgren for the next hand.

North
♠ 10 8 5 3 2
♡ 10 5 3 2
◊ K 5
♣ K 5

West
♠ K
♡ J 9 8
◊ J 7 6 3 2
♣ 7 6 4 2

East
♠ A J 9
♡ Q 7 6 4
◊ A 10 9
♣ J 10 9

South
♠ Q 7 6 4
♡ A K
◊ Q 8 4
♣ A Q 8 3

Both vulnerable.
Dealer South.

South	North
1NT	2♣
2♠	3♠
4♠	Pass

West leads the three of diamonds and, whether the king is played from dummy or not, East does best to take his ace while he can. South wins the heart return, crosses to the king of clubs and plays a small spade.

Suppose to begin with that East makes the natural play of the nine. South is sure to play low from hand, knowing that a singleton ace or king in the West hand is more likely than a singleton jack. Subsequently South will lead spades again from the table and lose only two tricks in the suit.

But suppose that on the first round of spades East

puts in the jack, a play that cannot possibly cost a trick. Now declarer has to consider the possibility that the jack is a singleton as well as the possibility that West has a singleton nine. South is virtually certain to cover the jack with his queen, thus losing three spade tricks and his contract.

There are many other situations where it pays to play the jack from J 9.

<pre>
              Q 10 8 4 3
K 7 6 2   J 9
              A 5
</pre>

Needing to hold his losses to one trick in the suit, South starts with the ace. If East drops the nine, declarer will have no option but to play the queen on the next round since a doubleton king in the East hand is no use to him. But if East drops the jack a losing option immediately appears. Declarer is quite likely to continue with a finesse of the eight.

<pre>
              Q 10 8 4 3
J 7 6   K 9 2
              A 5
</pre>

This is the corollary to the previous position. When South starts with the ace, East should drop the nine in an attempt to persuade declarer that his only chance is to play the queen on the second round.

Another position where it can hardly cost to play the jack from J 9 is the following.

<pre>
              A Q 6 5 2
J 9   K 7 4
              10 8 3
</pre>

When South leads the three West should put in the jack. If South believes this to be a singleton, he will finesse the eight on the next round thus losing a second trick in the suit.

One of the great masters of deception is Martin Hoffman who has a formidable reputation on the European tournament circuit. Hoffman has the happy knack of being able to think and play at great speed, and many a player has come to grief when trying to match his pace. Watch Hoffman in the East seat on this hand from a pairs tournament.

North
- ♠ A K Q 2
- ♡ A 10 8 3
- ◊ Q 8 2
- ♣ A 5

West
- ♠ 9 4
- ♡ K 2
- ◊ A K J 9 7 6
- ♣ J 10 2

East
- ♠ J 10 8 3
- ♡ J 9 6
- ◊ 10 3
- ♣ 9 7 6 3

South
- ♠ 7 6 5
- ♡ Q 7 5 4
- ◊ 5 4
- ♣ K Q 8 4

Neither vulnerable.
Dealer West.

West	North	East	South
1 ◊	Double	Pass	1 ♡
Pass	3 ♡	Pass	4 ♡
Pass	Pass	Pass	

West cashed his top diamonds and shifted to the jack of clubs. The declarer won with the ace and played the queen of diamonds from the table, inviting Hoffman to weaken his trump holding. Hoffman declined, discarding a club, and South had to decide how to tackle the trumps.

On the bidding it seemed certain that West had the king of hearts: the only question was whether it was once or twice guarded. Declarer played the ace of hearts followed by the three, and on the second round Hoffman nonchalantly played the jack. It looked as though West had started with K 9 2 in hearts and South happily covered with the queen. His happiness dissolved a moment later when a further diamond lead from West enabled East to score the nine of hearts *en passant.*

Clearly if Hoffman had made the routine play of the nine of hearts on the second round, the declarer would have played low and the defenders would have been held to three tricks.

A J 9 6 5

Q 10 7   K 4 3

8 2

In this standard position when South plays from hand West should put up the queen. If he plays the seven, declarer can finesse the nine to force out the king and subsequently pick up the entire suit with a second finesse.

The play of the queen is the correct technical move to block the suit, but it also has deceptive overtones, for declarer may place West with K Q x, ducking in dummy and losing a subsequent finesse to the king. A capable declarer will probably stick with his original intention, winning the ace, returning to hand in another suit, and finessing the nine on the second round.

But this is a situation in which double bluff may well prevail. If South is an expert who knows you to be a capable defender, there is a good case for playing the seven from the West hand on the first round. Expecting you to play high from Q 10 7 or K 10 7, declarer may place you with K Q 7 and finesse dummy's jack.

The opposite situation would arise if you really held K Q 7.

```
              A J 9 6 5
K Q 7                        10 4 3
               8 2
```

Normally you would play low from West on the first round, expecting South to finesse the nine. But an expert declarer may instead finesse the jack, as we have seen, so there is a good case for playing the king or queen on the first round to try and give the impression that you have K 10 7 or Q 10 7.

The technical and psychological advantages of playing 'second hand high' are shown in this deal which was played some years ago at the Cannes Festival.

```
                    North
                    ♠  5 4
                    ♡  A K Q 7 2
                    ◇  A Q 6 2
                    ♣  5 4
West                                East
♠  10 9 3                           ♠  K Q J 8 2
♡  J 10 9 4 3                       ♡  8
◇  J 9 8                            ◇  K 7 5 4
♣  Q 3                              ♣  J 7 2
                    South
                    ♠  A 7 6
                    ♡  6 5
                    ◇  10 3
                    ♣  A K 10 9 8 6
```

Neither vulnerable.
Dealer North.

West	North	East	South
Stoppa	Garozzo	Roudinesco	Forquet
	1 ♡	1 ♠	2 ♣
Pass	2 ◊	Pass	2NT
Pass	3NT	Pass	Pass
Pass			

West led the ten of spades and the ace was held up until the third round. Crossing to the queen of hearts, declarer returned a club, intending to finesse into the safe hand. But Jean-Marc Roudinesco in the East seat was having none of that. He played the jack of clubs on the first round.

You see the terrible problem this created for Forquet? He won with the king, crossed to dummy again in hearts, and played another club. When East played low, South had to decide whether East was more likely to have Q J x or J x x. The odds favored playing for the drop *provided* that East could be relied upon always to play his honor from Q x x or J x x. Forquet knew Roudinesco to be a formidable opponent, but a lingering doubt remained in his mind. After much agonising, Forquet finessed the ten and lost his game.

As you can see, the contract would have been made in great comfort if East had played low on the first round of clubs.

Playing the Known Card

We have seen the importance for declarer of playing a card he is known to hold at the first opportunity, and the principle is equally valid in defense. When a defender is marked with a particular card he must get rid of it as soon as he can, for declarer will not go wrong until he has seen it played. Here is a common position.

                    K 9 6 5
8 7 3   Q 10 2
                    A J 4

Declarer leads low from dummy, finesses the jack successfully and continues with the ace. East must drop the queen, the card he is known to hold, under the ace. South then has to decide between playing for the drop and finessing the nine on the third round. He has no problem if the queen does not appear.

                    A Q 8 7 3
K J 9 2   10 6 4
                    5

Needing to develop this side suit before drawing trumps, South finesses the queen and then takes a discard on the ace. West should not fail to drop the king, the card he is known to hold, under the ace. Until the king appears South knows that he can ruff low without risk.

The most cogent reason for playing the card you are known to hold is to protect partner's honors. In the diagrams that follow, the false card should be automatic but this is not the case except in expert circles.

                    7 6 3
A K   J 9 2
                    Q 10 8 5 4

Declarer leads a low card from dummy and the ten draws the king. When the suit is next led from dummy East must play the jack, the card he is known to hold, in an attempt to persuade South to go wrong. If East plays the nine, South will see that he has nothing to lose by ducking, for he must always lose three tricks if the king was a singleton.

Here is another common case.

	7 5 4	
K Q		10 8 2
	A J 9 6 3	

On the first round a finesse of the nine loses to West. When the suit is again led from dummy East has to play the ten, the card he is known to hold, in order to protect his partner's remaining high card. If East weakly plays the eight, South will realise that his only chance of avoiding a second loser is to go up with the ace.

West has to be alert to protect his partner's honor in the next situation.

	A Q 10 8 6 2	
J 5 3		K 7
	9 4	

Playing a notrump contract without a side entry in dummy, declarer needs to establish this suit. He starts by running the nine and has no problem if East takes his king. Suppose East is made of sterner stuff and calmly plays the seven. Hot defense, but it will do East no good unless West co-operates by playing the jack on the next round. If the jack does not appear South may well go up with the ace, for he has no chance of establishing the suit if West started with K J 5 3.

Playing the known card can be particularly vital at pairs, where every trick is important.

```
              ♠ A 9 7 6 4
              ♡ K J 3
              ◇ 5 4 2
♠ K J 5       ♣ A Q          ♠ Q 10 2
♡ Q 10 9 7 2                 ♡ A 5
◇ 9                          ◇ K J 8 3
♣ K 9 6 4     ♠ 8 3          ♣ 10 8 5 2
              ♡ 8 6 4
              ◇ A Q 10 7 6
              ♣ J 7 3
```

Match-point pairs.
East-West vulnerable.
Dealer North.

West	North	East	South
	1 ♠	Pass	1NT
Pass	Pass	Pass	

West leads the ten of hearts to the jack and ace. Declarer wins the heart return with the king and plays a diamond for a finesse of the ten. He then finesses the queen of clubs successfully and plays another diamond.

It's crunch time for East. He is known to have the jack of diamonds and he must not fail to play it, offering South an attractive losing option. South is likely to take the bait, covering with the queen in the hope of making nine easy tricks. In practice this will hold him to three diamonds and seven tricks altogether.

If East plays a feeble eight of diamonds on the second round, South will realise that nine tricks cannot be made and will play low. The duck keeps open his communications and makes sure of eight tricks.

The principle of playing the known card can usefully be extended to include playing a card you will shortly be known to hold. In the pairs game a trick can some-times be stolen if a poorly placed honor is played on the first round.

```
                    ♠ 5 2
                    ♡ 9 8 3
                    ◇ K Q 4
                    ♣ A Q J 6 2
♠ K 10 8 3                          ♠ Q 9 6 4
♡ J 5 4                             ♡ Q 10 7 2
◇ 10 8 5 2                          ◇ 9 6
♣ K 7                              ♣ 10 8 3
                    ♠ A J 7
                    ♡ A K 6
                    ◇ A J 7 3
                    ♣ 9 5 4
```

Match-point pairs.

Both vulnerable.

Dealer South.

South	North
1NT	3NT

West leads the three of spades to the queen and ace. At trick two South plays a club from hand. West can see that his king is doomed, and there can be few tricks for the defense in view of that strong dummy. The king of clubs should hit the table without pause for reflexion.

At once a losing option appears for declarer. He can either try for twelve tricks at the risk of making only ten when the club king is a singleton, or he can play safe for eleven tricks by allowing the club king to hold. If the 'doomed' king of clubs wins a trick after all, West will naturally waste no time in cashing his second king.

If West plays low to the first club, declarer will take the finesse and rake in twelve tricks without breathing hard.

A defender may be marked with a certain card by the bidding rather than by the play.

```
              ♠  10 9 3
              ♡  A 9 2
              ♦  9 6 3
              ♣  10 7 6 2
♠  J 7 4                        ♠  6
♡  K 6                          ♡  J 10 7 4
♦  K J 8 2                      ♦  Q 10 7 5 4
♣  A K J 9                      ♣  8 4 3
              ♠  A K Q 8 5 2
              ♡  Q 8 5 3
              ♦  A
              ♣  Q 5
```

Both vulnerable.
Dealer West.

West	North	East	South
1NT*	Pass	2◊	Double
3◊	Pass	Pass	3♠
Pass	4♠	Pass	Pass
Pass			

16-18

West cashes two top clubs and then leads the two of diamonds to the queen and ace. After drawing trumps on which East discards two diamonds, South has to read the heart position to lose only one trick in the suit.

West is marked with the king of hearts and declarer has no chance unless it is a doubleton king. The winning play, when South leads a low heart and West plays the six, is to insert the nine of hearts from dummy. East wins the trick, but the king falls on the second round and declarer has a marked finesse for the contract.

The play does not vary if West's king is accompanied by an honor instead of a small card. When the jack or the ten appears on the first round South still plays the nine from dummy, retaining the ace as an entry for the third-round finesse.

But see the difference it makes if West plays the king of hearts, the card he is known to hold, on the first round. Now South has to take a view. If he decides that West's second heart is a small card, he must win with the ace and return the two of hearts to his eight. If he places West with the jack or ten, he can either play the nine of hearts from dummy as before or win with the ace and return the two to his queen.

The play of the king of hearts on the first round creates a guess where there was no guess before, and that is what good defense is all about.

Chapter 3

SLIPPERY SPOTS

We were concerned in the first chapter with the deceptive use of honor cards. Choosing the right honor to play, while vitally important, is not enough to make you a tricky declarer. The experienced player achieves many of his best effects by the manner in which he handles his spot cards.

Most players are aware of the possibility of intercepting and scrambling the enemy signals. The best opportunities arise in those situations where the defenders have to rely heavily on the information they receive from each other.

```
              Q 7 3
A K 10 8 4              J 9 5
              6 2
```

Against your trump contract West leads the king of a suit he has mentioned in the bidding and East follows with the five. If you play the two, West will realise that his partner has played the lowest of three cards and will shift to another suit. But if you drop the six under the king, West may be persuaded that his partner has started an echo to show a doubleton and may continue the suit to your advantage.

The opposite situation is shown in the next diagram.

```
              Q 7 3
A K 10 8 4              5
              J 9 6 2
```

This time you must drop the two under the king to leave open for West the possibility that his partner started with J 9 5. West may still do the right thing, of course, reasoning that with 6 2 you would have played the six and not the two. The possibilities of bluff and counter-bluff are endless, but one thing is sure. You have no chance of avoiding a ruff in the suit if you play any card other than the two.

Clearly it would be a giveaway if you took time to think in these situations. You need to be able to make your play automatically, and fortunately there is a simple rule to follow. Act as declarer exactly as you would if you were a defender: that is to say, start an echo when you wish to induce a continuation and play your lowest card when you want a shift. This rule applies when normal defensive signals are in use. If your opponets are using reverse signals, common in Scandinavia and elsewhere, you must reverse your own tactics.

Rich rewards can be reaped at notrumps if you can persuade a defender that his partner has played an encouraging card.

9 5 4

K led   8 played

J 10 6 3

You know that East's eight is likely to be a singleton, but if you drop the six from hand West may continue the suit and make it easy for you to establish a trick.

8 4 2

Q led   7 played

A K 6 5 3

Suppose you are lucky enough to attract a lead in a suit that you have concealed in the bidding. If you win the first trick and return the suit, you give the enemy a chance to shift their attack. But if you play the five on the first round, West is likely to continue, putting you a tempo ahead. Note that the right card in these situations is always the second lowest. To drop the six would be overdoing things, since West might start to wonder about the two lower cards that are missing. You are trying to convince him that his partner has K 7 3.

	K 6	
J 9 5 3		10 7
	A Q 8 4 2	

Again in this position you can take advantage of an attack on your concealed suit. When West leads the three, play the six from dummy and give East a green light by dropping the four under his ten. East is almost sure to continue the suit, presenting you with a tempo.

It is not only when following suit that you have to choose your small cards with care. The cards you lead towards dummy can be equally important. When there is a long suit on the table the defenders will normally give count signals, and there is no reason why you should not gatecrash the party.

	K Q 10 7	
J 9 5		A 8 4 2
	6 3	

In tackling this suit your aim is to smoke out the ace if East has it, for that will make the subsequent play easier for you. For the best chance of success, lead the six to dummy's queen, concealing the three. East may be reluctant to hold off, fearing that his partner may have started an echo from J 9 5 3.

At notrumps, where there are no outside entries in

dummy, it is often possible to steal a second trick in a position like the following.

```
              K Q J 7 4
10 6 5                          A 9 8
              3 2
```

Play the three to dummy's jack, which will be allowed to win. When you continue with the king from the table East may hold up his ace a second time, placing his partner with 5 2.

```
              K Q J 8 3
6 5                             A 9 4
              10 7 2
```

In this situation you want to persuade East to take his ace on the second round. The only way to give yourself a chance is to play the two to dummy's jack. On the second round East will have to decide whether his partner's six is the start of an echo or the lowest card from 10 7 6.

```
              K Q 10 9

              J 6 2
```

Again there is no side entry in dummy and you would like the defenders to take their ace on the second round. How you tackle the suit depends in this case on your estimate of who holds the missing ace, for the second round of the suit must be played through that defender.

If you think West has the ace, start with the jack and follow with the six on the second round. West may believe his partner to have started an echo to show four cards in the suit, in which case he will see no reason to hold up again.

The suit has to be handled differently if you place the ace with East. Lead the six for a 'finesse' of the nine and continue with the king. If East, holding A x x, is persuaded that his partner started with J x x x, he may take his ace on the second round.

Even when you have no specific purpose in mind, it is usually a good idea to sow a little confusion when you cross from hand to hand.

A K 7

Q 4 2

When entering dummy in this suit, lead the four rather than the two, especially if you have reason to fear an attack in another suit. Each defender may believe the other to be echoing and either may return the suit when he gains the lead.

It may even be possible to persuade both defenders that you are taking a finesse.

A Q J 2

K 5 3

Entering dummy in order to tackle another suit, lead the five to dummy's jack. West may think that his partner is holding up and echoing, while East may credit his partner with the king and place you with high cards that you do not possess in other suits. A small deception like this can bring unexpected benefits.

Defenders rely greatly on honest count signals from each other in two situations. (1) When dummy has no entry except in the suit that declarer is playing, and (2) in the early stages of the play when declarer's distribution is still unclear. Once they know more about the hand their signals can no longer be relied on, for they will be concerned mainly with confusing the issue.

One way of taking advantage of the defenders' need to exchange honest information is shown in the following deal.

```
                    ♠ 7 6 3
                    ♡ 8 5 3
                    ◇ K Q 8 4
                    ♣ 7 3 2
  ♠ K 9 5                        ♠ A 10 8
  ♡ Q J 10 6 4                   ♡ 9 7 2
  ◇ 10 6 2                       ◇ J 9 3
  ♣ Q 8                          ♣ 10 9 6 4
                    ♠ Q J 4 2
                    ♡ A K
                    ◇ A 7 5
                    ♣ A K J 5
```

Both vulnerable.
Dealer South.

South	North
2NT	3NT

Against this standard contract West leads the queen of hearts to the three, two and king. The hearts appear to be 5-3, which means that you lack the tempo to establish spade tricks and must rely on the minor suits.

But you are in a bit of a quandary. If the diamonds are good for four tricks you will need only three tricks from the clubs, and the best way to try for three tricks in clubs is to cash the ace and king and then play a third round from dummy towards your jack. There is no guarantee that the diamonds will break, however. If you have only three tricks in diamonds you will need to try for four clubs by finessing against the queen. How do you know which line to choose?

The answer is to let the opponents tell you. Play a

low diamond to dummy's queen at trick two. The defenders are sure to yield honest information at this stage, since for all each of them knows his partner may have the diamond ace. When both defenders follow with their lowest cards, you know what to do in clubs. You cash the ace and king, and the fall of the queen solves all your problems. If the queen had not appeared, you would have cashed three more diamonds, discarding a spade from hand, before playing a club towards your jack.

If the defenders had started echoes on the first round of diamonds, you would have known that you needed four tricks from the clubs. After cashing the club ace and the remaining top diamonds (just in case), you would have played a club from dummy for a second-round finesse.

This simple type of anti-deception play is often missed. I hope you appreciate that there is no way the defenders will give out honest signals if you start with the ace of diamonds. That tells them too much too soon, and they will put on a false-carding act.

Most of the deceptions we have considered so far have been concerned with masking strength in a suit. Disguising weakness is not so easy, but you can sometimes frighten an opponent off by making a show of strength.

8 7 2

Q 5

If East at some point leads a low card in this suit, don't make it easy for the defense by playing low. Put up the queen and perhaps West will shift, thinking you have a further honor in the suit.

J 7 5

Q 10 8 4 3   A 9 2

K 6

When West leads the four to his partner's ace, try the effect of dropping the king. East may be persuaded that you hold the queen as well and direct his attack elsewhere.

K led

<pre>
        Q 6

        10 7 3
</pre>

This looks fairly hopeless when West leads the king. But if you calmly 'unblock' the queen from dummy West may think twice about continuing.

Good defenders may be deceived in positions like the following.

<pre>
            J 5
K Q 8 3   A 9 4
          10 7 6 2
</pre>

Suppose that East, having won the first trick in another suit against your notrump contract, finds the deadly shift to the nine of this suit. It is the only card that allows the defense to take four fast tricks in the suit, but it has the drawback of being none too easy to read. You can take advantage of this, when West wins with the queen, by 'unblocking' the jack from dummy. West is virtually certain to place you with the ace as well as the ten, and his shift will bring welcome relief.

Exploiting Fears

Declarer's big advantage is that he is always aware of the exact strength ranged against him in each suit. This is not the case for the defenders, who do not possess x-ray vision and who have to guess, at least in the early stages, about the declarer's holding in any particular suit.

There are many positions in which declarer can exploit the ignorance and the fears of his right-hand opponent by playing a small card from dummy towards his hand.

```
              K 7 4 3
J 9 5                        A 10 6 2
              Q 8
```

You are playing in a trump contract and need to develop this side suit. Naturally you start with a low card from the table and East, holding the ace, has an immediate guess to make. He may be tempted to play his ace in case you have a singleton queen. This would immediately give you a second trick in the suit. Suppose East plays low and your queen wins. Now the technical chance is to duck on the way back, hoping to establish a second trick if East began with no more than three cards in the suit. However, if entries permit, it is much better to cross to dummy in another suit and play a further small card from the table. Lacking the jack, East will again be under tremendous pressure and may well play his ace on air.

It can be right to tackle a suit in this manner even when you have no legitimate chance of success.

```
              K 8 7 4
Q 10 6 2                     A 9 5 3
              J
```

Normally you would lead the jack from hand, hoping to find the ace with West. But if you know from the bidding that East must have the ace, try the effect of leading the four from dummy. East may go up with the ace for fear of allowing you to make a singleton queen.

```
              8 5
Q 6                          A 10 9 3
              K J 7 4 2
```

Again you are playing in a trump contract and need tricks from this side suit. When you lead from dummy and East plays low, you make the right guess by putting up the king. With plenty of entries to dummy you should avoid the lazy play of a small card from hand on the next round. Return to dummy and play the second round from the table to make East reach for the aspirin bottle.

The next diagram shows another situation where it is possible to put East under heavy pressure. It is a common position which you will meet over and over again at the table.

A Q 7 6

J 10 8 3   K 9 2

5 4

Needing two tricks from this suit, many players would see no alternative to the finesse. However, if you can afford to lose a trick in the suit, it is far better to start with a low card from the table. The finesse can always be tried on the next round, but meanwhile East may solve your problems by going up with the king. He could not be censured too heavily if he did, for if you held J x in the suit it would be fatal for him to duck. After winning the jack you would return to the ace and ruff out his king on the third round, ending up with three tricks to his none.

Here is another common position.

Q 10 6 4

J

Again you are in a trump contract and this is one of your side suits. The best chance of establishing a trick for yourself without losing two tricks in the suit is to start with a low card from dummy. If the honors are divided it will not be easy for East to go up on the first round, especially if he has the king. If West wins the first trick, you can subsequently take a ruffing finesse against East to set up your trick.

It is not so easy to play on the nerves of your left-hand opponent, for you have to play in front of him and the sight of dummy usually clarifies the position for him. Still, it is by no means impossible to put an honor card to sleep.

<pre>
                    9
A 7 6 4   8 5 2
               K Q J 10 3
</pre>

Needing to avoid a loser in this side suit, you would naturally start with the three from hand. If West declines to waste his ace on the lowly nine he will wind up with a pair of red ears.

A good swindle of this type occurred in the Budapest heat of the Philip Morris European Cup in 1980, and I am indebted to Martin Hoffman for the report. Watch Julian Klukowski of Poland, current European Champion, hacking out of the rough to get his birdie.

<pre>
                    ♠ J 5 2
                    ♡ A 10 9 6
                    ◇ 10 9
  ♠ 10 8 4   ♣ K J 8 4   ♠ A Q 9 3
  ♡ K 8 3   ♡ Q 7 5
  ◇ K 8 5 4   ◇ 6 3
  ♣ Q 6 5   ♠ K 7 6   ♣ 10 9 7 3
                    ♡ J 4 2
                    ◇ A Q J 7 2
                    ♣ A 2
</pre>

Match-point pairs.
Neither vulnerable.
Dealer West.

West	North	East	South
Pass	Pass	Pass	1NT
Pass	2♣	Pass	2♦
Pass	3NT	Pass	Pass
Pass			

A spade was the popular lead from the West hand and the declarers normally made nine tricks on the nose, losing three spades and a diamond.

Against Klukowski West led the three of hearts and East, on winning with the queen, found the deadly shift to the queen of spades. In theory the contract was now doomed, but Klukowski showed no signs of alarm. He won the king of spades and promptly played the two of diamonds. This play was likely to bring in at least ten tricks if East held the diamond king, and it offered an extra chance when the diamond finesse was wrong. Sure enough, West saw no reason to go up with his king and the nine of diamonds won the trick.

The rest was plain sailing. Declarer returned to hand with the ace of clubs, ran the jack of hearts and cashed two more heart tricks. Reading the position well, he returned to the ace of diamonds and finessed the jack of clubs. Finally, adding insult to injury, he threw East in with the fourth round of clubs, thus scoring a tenth trick with the jack of spades.

West must pick up the tab for allowing declarer to make ten tricks instead of eight. Knowing that his partner had spade tricks to cash, West should of course have played the king of diamonds on the first round of the suit. But the point is that all players, even good players, will sometimes go wrong if given the opportunity to do so.

Chapter 4

DUCKING TO DECEIVE

Perhaps the most potent of all the weapons in the hands of the defenders is the hold-up, which has deceptive as well as technical merits. Defenders who are persuaded to part with their aces and kings at the first opportunity make life easy for the experienced declarer. With the location of the enemy honors clarified at an early stage, the declarer can plan the play to make the most of his technical chances.

It is a different story if the defenders refuse to release their high cards. After several tricks declarer is likely to have serious problems, for he may have to commit himself to a particular line of play while still unsure of the location of the enemy honors. In such circumstances he is bound to do the wrong thing some of the time.

The simplest form of hold-up, known to all players and practiced by most, is shown in the following diagram.

```
              K Q 10 7
J 9 3                        A 8 2
              6 5 4
```

South leads a small card and plays the king from dummy. Normally it will be right for East to hold up, playing the two without undue haste or delay but in measured tempo. If East plays the ace he leaves South no alternative to the winning play of finessing the ten on the second round.

                    K Q 10 7
A 9 3   J 8 2
                    6 5 4

Similarly, in the above diagram West should play low on the first round and low again on the second round. If the defenders have given nothing away by their manner, declarer is bound to get it wrong sometimes.

                    A Q J 4
10 5 3   K 9 2
                    8 7 6

In this case, when declarer finesses dummy's jack, East should steel himself to play low without a flicker. South may then base his plan of campaign on the assumption that the finesse is right. Note that it is the play of the three by West on the first round, indicating an odd number of cards in the suit, that makes it safe for East to duck if this is a side suit in a trump contract.

It is rather more dangerous to hold up in the West seat when declarer leads a small card from dummy and plays an honor from his hand.

                    7 5 4
K 10 3   9 6 2
                    A Q J 8

A low card is led from the table for a finesse of the queen (or the jack). The hold-up is not entirely without risk, but if this is an early play in a notrump contract it is not likely that declarer has led towards an unsupported honor. The chance of gain far outweighs the risk of loss for the hold-up.

Look at what happened on this hand.

```
                    ♠ 9 4 3
                    ♡ K 7
                    ◇ A K J 10
                    ♣ A 9 4 2
♠ K 10 8 5                                    ♠ 7 2
♡ 10 9 8 3                                    ♡ J 6 5 4 2
◇ 7 6 2                                       ◇ 9 5 3
♣ 8 5                                         ♣ Q 10 6
                    ♠ A Q J 6
                    ♡ A Q
                    ◇ Q 8 4
                    ♣ K J 7 3
```

Both vulnerable.
Dealer South.

South	North
1♣	1◇
2NT	3♣
3NT	4NT
6NT	Pass

Declarer won the opening heart lead in hand, entered dummy with a diamond and played a spade to his queen, which held the trick. Counting on three tricks in spades and six tricks in the red suits, he decided that he required only three tricks from clubs.

South knew the appropriate safety play. He cashed the king of clubs and continued with a small one, covering the eight with dummy's nine. East won and knocked out the last heart stopper. After cashing his other winners South confidently repeated the spade finesse and was shattered when West produced the king to defeat the contract.

West defended well but a more experienced declarer

would have landed the slam. It was correct to test the spades first, but South's assumption that the king was well placed when the finesse won was altogether too innocent. It costs nothing to return to dummy and repeat the finesse. West has to take his king on the second round, and South now knows that he needs four tricks from the clubs.

It takes strong nerves to hold up when in doing so you unguard an honor card. Such a hold-up can be most effective and is usually described as 'brilliant' when it succeeds.

                    A K J 9
    8 6 4 3   Q 7 2
                    10 5

Declarer is playing in notrumps and dummy has no outside entries. When South runs the ten, East may bring off a coup by playing the two with the right degree of unconcern. In a pairs game, where every overtrick counts, declarer is almost sure to repeat the finesse, thus holding himself to one trick in the suit.

                    A Q J 10 5
    9 8 6 4   K 2
                    7 3

This is a similar case. If East has the nerve to play low when the ten is finessed, declarer is likely to return to hand in another suit and finesse again.

Baring an honor card is much less dangerous than it looks, for it is hard for declarer to believe that you have done such a thing. The contract does not have to be notrumps, and it is not necessary for dummy to be short of entries for this sort of play to gain.

Here is a hand from the Scottish Trials of some years ago.

```
                    ♠ A 5
                    ♡ A Q J
                    ◇ A K 8 3
                    ♣ Q 8 6 5
♠ 10 9 6                              ♠ Q 7 2
♡ 10 5 4                              ♡ K 3
◇ Q 10 9 5 2                          ◇ 7 4
♣ 9 3                                ♣ K J 10 7 4 2
                    ♠ K J 8 4 3
                    ♡ 9 8 7 6 2
                    ◇ J 6
                    ♣ A
```

North-South vulnerable.
Dealer South.

South	North
Pass	1♣ *
1♠	2NT
3♡	3NT
4♡	5◇
6♡	Pass

Precision

Most pairs were content to play in game on this deal, but at one table South had taken too much porage for his breakfast. Six hearts is not the greatest of contracts, with chances of something under 30%, but on the lie of the cards it seemed destined to succeed.

South won the opening club lead and played a heart for a finesse of the jack. In the East seat was John Mac-Laren--never one to submit meekly to the whims of destiny. He calmly played the three of hearts under dummy's jack. Naturally South returned to hand with a club ruff to repeat the trump finesse. Now you can see what happened. The king of hearts won, and a third round of clubs enabled West to score the setting trick with the ten of hearts.

One of the best swindles of this type on record was perpetrated many years ago in the South American Championships.

```
                    ♠ A 6 3
                    ♥ 9 7 6
                    ◇ 7 3
                    ♣ A K J 5 3
  ♠ J 10 9 5 4                      ♠ Q 8
  ♥ 3                               ♥ A K J 10 5 4
  ◇ Q 9 2                           ◇ 6 5
  ♣ Q 10 7 4       ♠ K 7 2         ♣ 8 6 2
                    ♥ Q 8 2
                    ◇ A K J 10 8 4
                    ♣ 9
```

North-South vulnerable.
Dealer South.

South	West	North	East
1 ◇	1 ♠	2 ♣	2 ♥
Pass	Pass	3 ♣	Pass
3 ◇	Pass	3 ♠	Pass
3NT	Pass	Pass	Pass

The jack of spades was led and the declarer won with the ace in order to take an immediate diamond finesse. West, Roberto Benaim of Venezuela, calmly dropped the nine of diamonds under the ten, and declarer can hardly be blamed for imagining that all was plain sailing. After crossing to the ace of clubs and discarding his spade loser on the club king, South repeated the diamond finesse.

Now the roof fell in. West produced the queen of diamonds and cashed the queen of clubs. In order to keep his heart guard South was compelled to discard a winning diamond from hand. A further spade lead put

South in to cash his diamonds, but he had to concede three heart tricks to East at the end.

In the classic book, 'Why You Lose at Bridge,' Skid Simon listed the premature winning of tricks as one of the prime sources of loss to the defense. He advised his readers to start ducking their aces but to consider that they had graduated only after a successful duck in a small slam when a singleton had been led from dummy.

There are many technical reasons for ducking, but here we are concerned only with the psychological aspects. Declarer is likely to go wrong if he has a guess to make in the suit.

I used the following hand in 'Match-Point Bridge' but it is worth another airing.

```
              ♠ 3
              ♡ 9 8 6 3
              ◇ A Q J 8 4
              ♣ J 9 6
♠ Q 8 5 4                    ♠ A 7 6 2
♡ J 7                        ♡ 5 2
◇ 7 2                        ◇ 10 9 6 5 3
♣ K Q 10 5 4                 ♣ 7 3
              ♠ K J 10 9
              ♡ A K Q 10 4
              ◇ K
              ♣ A 8 2
```

Match-point pairs.

Both vulnerable.
Dealer South.

South	North
1♡	3♡
4NT	5◇
6♡	Pass

The lead of the king of clubs goes to South's ace. Declarer cashes two top hearts and the king of diamonds, then enters dummy with a heart to the nine, West discarding a club and East a spade. On the top diamonds declarer throws two clubs and a spade, while West parts with a card in each black suit.

While all this is going on, East has to make up his mind about what he is going to do when the singleton spade is led from the table. A complete count of the hand is available. Declarer is marked with five hearts, one diamond, three clubs and therefore four spades, one of which he has already discarded. Since dummy has only one trump available for ruffing spades, there is no danger of allowing declarer to make all thirteen tricks. If East calmly plays low when the singleton spade is led, declarer is almost sure to take a losing finesse to West's queen, after which a spade return will defeat the slam.

When the hand was played in a tournament most of the declarers were not tested, for the East players lacked the courage to play low when the singleton spade was led from dummy.

A hold-up can pay big dividends in situations like the following.

A Q J 10 3

8 4   K 9 7 2

6 5

Declarer is playing in a trump contract and needs to develop this side suit. If East takes his king when the ten is finessed, he releases the rest of the suit for declarer's use. But if he plays low, declarer will cash the ace and ruff on the third round. Even if West is not in a position to over-ruff, declarer may no longer be able to establish the suit.

$$Q\ 5$$
$$10\ 3 \qquad\qquad K\ 8\ 6\ 2$$
$$A\ J\ 9\ 7\ 4$$

This time the contract is notrumps and declarer tackles the suit by playing low from hand to dummy's queen. If East wins the king it is likely to be the only trick in the suit for the defense. But if East nonchalantly plays the two under the queen, declarer will be tempted to finesse the nine on the way back, thus allowing the defenders two tricks in the suit.

Curious effects can be produced when a defender refuses to do the obvious thing with an honor card. On the following hand the declarer was persuaded to go down in a cold slam.

```
                    ♠ A 5
                    ♡ A 7 5 2
                    ◇ K J 9 8 4
    ♠ 6 3 2         ♣ 9 7          ♠ 8
    ♡ K 6 3                        ♡ Q J 10 9 4
    ◇ A 10 5 3                     ◇ 7 6 2
    ♣ 8 5 2         ♠ K Q J 10 9 7 4  ♣ K J 6 3
                    ♡ 8
                    ◇ Q
                    ♣ A Q 10 4
```

Neither vulnerable.
Dealer North.

West	North	East	South
	1 ◇	1 ♡	2 ♠
Pass	3 ◇	Pass	3 ♠
Pass	4 ♡	Pass	4NT
Pass	5 ♡	Pass	6 ♠
Pass	Pass	Pass	

West led the three of hearts to dummy's ace. Not wishing to stake everything on the club finesse, South played a small diamond from the table and was gratified when his queen held the trick. Seeing a way of avoiding the club finesse, he continued with a low club to the nine. East won with the jack and returned his spade to dummy's ace.

Convinced that the ace of diamonds was on his right, South played the king of diamonds and ran it, discarding a club from hand. But West produced the ace of diamonds and returned the six of spades to put the slam two down.

Note that South could not have gone wrong if West had taken his ace of diamonds at trick two. After winning the second trump in dummy, South would have discarded two clubs on winning diamonds and finessed in clubs for his twelfth trick.

Are you convinced by now that holding up honor cards is a worth-while pastime? What about this situation?

```
                K 5
   J 10                        A 8 3
            Q 9 7 6 4 2
```

Needing to restrict his losers to one trick in the suit, South plays a low card to dummy's king. The position is really a fugitive from the 'obligatory false cards'. If East takes his ace, declarer will have no option to play for the drop on the second round. If East holds off, however, South will place West with A J or A 10 doubleton and duck on the way back, permitting the defenders to score two tricks.

Let us alter the position slightly to give West an extra card in the suit.

```
                K 5
   J 10 4                      A 8 3
            Q 9 7 6 2
```

Now it looks as though it could cost the defenders a trick if East holds off when a low card is played to the king. In theory this is undeniable, but in practice it never happens. When the king wins, declarer ducks on the way back and the defenders make their two tricks anyway. This sort of hold-up can be vital at notrumps when East needs to preserve an entry until his side suit is established.

An example of the play cropped up when Great Britain met Poland in the 1981 European Championships.

```
                    ♠ K 8 4 2
                    ♡ K J 4 3
                    ◇ 10 6 4
  ♠ Q J 7 6 3       ♣ Q 2
  ♡ 9 7 5                        ♠ 10 9
  ◇ 8 5                          ♡ Q 8 6
  ♣ J 9 4                        ◇ K Q 9 7 3
                    ♠ A 5        ♣ A 10 8
                    ♡ A 10 2
                    ◇ A J 2
                    ♣ K 7 6 5 3
```

North-South vulnerable.
Dealer East.

Open Room	South Collings	West Martens	North Hackett	East Przybora
				1◇
	1NT	Pass	2NT	Pass
	3NT	Pass	Pass	Pass
Closed Room	Milde	Rose	Kudla	Sheehan
				Pass
	1NT	Pass	2♡	Dblc
	3♣	Pass	3◇	Pass
	3NT	Pass	Pass	Pass

The bid of one diamond in the Open Room did not necessarily promise length in the suit, so West chose a spade as his opening lead. This posed no great problems and John Collings brought home nine tricks by establishing the clubs.

In the Closed Room Irving Rose led a diamond in response to his partner's double of the 'Forcing Stayman' bid of two diamonds. North and East played low and declarer won the trick with the jack. When a club was led to the queen, Rob Sheehan declined to part with his ace, dropping the eight without batting an eye. On the next round of clubs declarer naturally played low from hand, hoping for a doubleton ace with West. In with the ten of clubs, Sheehan continued with the king of diamonds to force out the ace. Still expecting West to have the club ace, declarer thought it best to play another club rather than try to guess the heart position. To his dismay, East produced the ace and cashed three diamonds to put the contract one down.

It was mentioned earlier that when you have made a first-round duck of this sort declarer will never think of playing high on the second round. The statement needs modification, for when an opponent knows you to be capable of this sort of duck he may well credit you with too much guile. This is typical of the sort of bonus that comes along when an occasional bluffer is wrongly suspected of bluffing. I remember with pleasure a hand from a pairs tournament where I received a top for doing nothing more clever than follow suit.

```
                     ♠ 9 8 3
                     ♡ K 4
                     ◇ Q 9 8 4 2
                     ♣ A Q 7
 ♠ Q 6 2                              ♠ K 10 7 5
 ♡ J 10 9 7 3                         ♡ Q 6 5
 ◇ J 10 5                             ◇ A 3
 ♣ 8 4                                ♣ 10 9 6 2
                     ♠ A J 4
                     ♡ A 8 2
                     ◇ K 7 6
                     ♣ K J 5 3
```

Match-point pairs.
Both vulnerable.
Dealer South.

South	North
1NT	3NT

No need to tell you who held the 4-count in the West seat. South was a player I had met once or twice, but North was a complete stranger.

My lead of the jack of hearts held the first trick and the second heart was won by the king, East unblocking his queen. Declarer played a diamond to his king and continued with a second diamond on which I played the ten. Declarer tranced and my hopes began to rise. Sure enough, he eventually went up with the queen from dummy. Partner took his ace and cleared the hearts, and there was no way for declarer to come to a ninth trick.

North became vocal as players do on these occasions.

'What an insane way to play the diamonds' he screeched. 'What on earth were you thinking about?'

South shrugged and explained that he thought I might have ducked with A 10 5. He had my sympathy, for it would, of course, have been good play for me to duck with this holding. If I had won the ace, declarer would have been able to establish the diamonds by ducking the second round to East, who would by then be out of hearts.

As my partner and I took our seats at the next table we heard a final scornful sally from North.

'Who did you think you were playing against? Terence Reese?'

Chapter 5

CRASH COURSE

One of the purest of life's pleasures comes from persuading opponents to win a trick twice over with their honor cards. There is no pleasure without pain, the philosophers tell us, but in this case the pain belongs exclusively to the defenders. Many a long-standing partnership has been broken up over the crashing of honors, and it is your duty and your pleasure to try and split up a few more.

9 7 5 4

K 6   A

Q J 10 8 3 2

With this holding in the trump suit you will naturally start with the queen from hand rather than a small card from dummy. This can be particularly effective if West has bid notrumps at some time in the auction. It is hard for him to judge the position and he may well go up with the king, colliding with his partner's ace. Would you never go up as West? In that case you will lose a trick when the position is as follows:

9 7 5 4

K 6   3

A Q J 10 8 2

Again declarer plays the queen from hand and West is faced with the same cruel dilemma.

Sometimes it will be East who has bid notrumps and can therefore be placed with length in the suit.

Q 6 3

A   K 10 8

J 9 7 5 4 2

Now you can play on East's nerves by starting with the queen from dummy. If East covers, the defenders make only one trick in the suit. It is all very well to say that East should not cover, but from his point of view the position could be as follows:

Q 6 3

9   K 10 8

A J 7 5 4 2

Knowing that East cannot have a singleton king, you again start with the queen from dummy. This time East loses a trick if he fails to cover.

J 4

Q 5 2   K 10

A 9 8 7 6 3

With this holding the technical chance of avoiding two losers is to start with a low card from hand, playing West for K 10 or Q 10 doubleton. If he wins the first trick, you can subsequently enter dummy and run the jack to pin his ten. Even if you have no entries to dummy a low card from hand is still the best play, for you put West under pressure when the situation is as above. It is hard for West to know what to do, since you would play the same way if you had AKxxxx in the suit.

J 6 5 4

A 9 7 3 2

In the absence of a 2-2 break, you would normally

expect to avoid two losers in this suit only if East has a singleton honor. But if a singleton in the East hand can be ruled out, it is better to start with the jack from dummy. This combines the technical possibility of pinning a singleton ten in the West hand with the chance that East may be tempted to cover from K 10 8 or Q 10 8.

Players clutching a broken sequence often feel an overwhelming urge to cover when an honor card or a high spot is led from dummy. Do not fail to exploit this automatic reflex in cases like the following.

10 5 2
J 9 8 6
A K Q 7 4 3

Naturally you don't expect to lose a trick in this suit, but if entries are plentiful it can cost nothing to start with the ten from dummy. You are not planning to run the ten, of course, but when the suit breaks badly as in the diagram East may save the day for you by covering with the jack.

9 6 4

Q   J 10 8 3

A K 7 5 2

In this combination you have nothing to lose by starting with the nine from the table. If East is persuaded to cover, you need lose only one trick in the suit.

This sort of deception can be just as effective in a side suit. Watch Pedro Paul Assumpcao of Brazil bringing home an impossible contract in the 1978 World Pairs Olympiad.

```
              ♠ Q 10 5 2
              ♡ A 4 3
              ◊ J 7 6
              ♣ A Q 2
♠ K 8 3                        ♠ J 6
♡ 10 8 6 5                     ♡ K Q J 9 2
◊ A                            ◊ K Q 8 4
♣ J 6 5 4 3                    ♣ 9 7
              ♠ A 9 7 4
              ♡ 7
              ◊ 10 9 5 3 2
              ♣ K 10 8
```

Match-point pairs.

Neither vulnerable.

Dealer North.

West	North	East	South
	1 ◊	1 ♡	1 ♠
3 ♡	3 ♠	4 ♡	4 ♠
Double	Pass	Pass	Pass

West led a heart, and Assumpcao must have been far from happy when dummy went down. There appeared to be three diamonds and at least one spade to lose, and it looked very much as though four hearts would have been defeated.

Giving no sign that he was in trouble, Assumpcao won the ace of hearts and played the jack of diamonds from the table. East covered with the queen and the defenders won the trick twice over. Now it was just a matter of keeping East off lead until trumps had been drawn. Declarer won the club return with the ace and ran the queen of spades to West's king. The next club was won with the queen, trumps were drawn, ending in dummy, and the play of another diamond completed East's misery.

Making four spades doubled was worth 76 match points out of 77 to Assumpcao and Chagas.

There is also a more subtle way of causing enemy honors to collide.

```
                    ♠ Q J 7 3
                    ♡ K Q
                    ◇ A 4
                    ♣ K Q 8 7 2
♠ A 6 4                              ♠ K
♡ 3                                  ♡ A 10 9 8 6 2
◇ J 9 6 5 2                          ◇ Q 10 8 3
♣ J 10 6 4                           ♣ 9 3
                    ♠ 10 9 8 5 2
                    ♡ J 7 5 4
                    ◇ K 7
                    ♣ A 5
```

North-South vulnerable.
Dealer North.

West	North	East	South
	1♣	1♡	1♠
Pass	3♠	Pass	4♠
Pass	Pass	Pass	

It seemed a reasonable enough game, but West led the three of hearts to his partner's ace, ruffed the heart return and shifted to the five of diamonds. Now the prospects looked bleak, for the defenders were due to collect the two top trumps to defeat the contract.

However, the declarer saw a way of putting West to the test. He won the ace of diamonds in dummy, entered his hand with the ace of clubs and led the jack of hearts. It was a seemingly pointless play, for a discard from dummy was of no use to him. But West could not know that. Thinking that South intended to discard the losing diamond from the table, West ruffed with his remaining small spade, and that was the end of the defense. South over-ruffed in dummy and played a trump to make the enemy honors knock heads.

Deceptive Finessing

Sometimes it is quickly apparent that the success of the contract will depend on a correct guess in the critical suit. It may be a fifty-fifty shot, but the player with a deceptive style usually manages to get better odds for his finesses.

K J 8 2

6 5

Suppose that your slam contract depends on taking the right view in this side suit. The best shot is to tackle the suit at trick two before West knows too much about the hand. West will be under considerable pressure to play the ace if he has it, since you may have a singleton and a loser elsewhere for all he knows. If West plays low, therefore, you should be inclined to finesse the jack.

The game becomes easier if you can persuade opponents to part with their high cards at an early stage, and there is quite an art in smoking out the enemy honors.

A Q 9 3

J 10 5

Here you want to discover the location of the king as soon as possible. If you run the jack you will be none the wiser, since East will hold up smoothly if he has the king. Provided that you can afford the blockage, it is better to lead the five to dummy's queen on the first round. Now East will be unlikely to hold up for fear of losing a trick in the suit.

7 6 2

K Q 10 4

Playing in notrumps, you lead this suit from dummy, hoping to discover who has the ace. The king is a good card to play against average defenders, for West is likely to take the ace if he has it, being unsure who has the queen. In an expert game, however, West is likely to hold up if you play the king, taking the view that you would not be leading towards an unsupported honor. It is not so easy for West to hold up if you play the queen, for he will be reluctant to concede an early tempo if his partner has the king.

6 5 4

A Q J 3

In this case a finesse of the queen will work satisfactorily against most defenders and will conceal your possession of the jack. But an expert West is more likely to take his king if you finesse the jack on the first round, for he will reason that his partner could have the ace.

When leading from a sequence of honors for a finesse, the choice of card must be influenced by whether you want your opponent to cover or not. The highest card is the one most likely to induce a cover, and the lowest will give you the best chance of slipping past the enemy honor.

K 8 4 3

J 10

Here you want West to play the ace if he has it, and it

would be foolish to lead the jack. West would just play low with a wooden face, hoping for you to run the jack. The ten is the right card to lead, for West may then think that you have no alternative to the winning play of putting up the king. If West plays low on the ten, therefore, the odds will favour running it.

A K J 4

10 9

Needing four tricks from this suit when there is no outside entry in dummy, lead the nine for the first finesse in the hope of slipping past the queen. If you start with the ten, West is likely to cover and block the suit.

Q 8 4

A 10 9 3

Suppose you have to tackle this suit from your own hand. Naturally you want West to play the king if he has it, and the best shot is to start with the three, concealing the fact that you have a choice of plays from dummy. If the king does not appear on your left, the odds will favour a finesse of the eight.

A 7 3

Q J 9

In this case you would like West to cover on the first round, and the queen is the right card to play. No doubt West should refuse to cover unless he has the ten as well as the king, but it is hard for defenders to be sure of doing the right thing in these situations. After all, you might be trying a 'fool's finesse' holding Q x.

A 7 2

Q J 10 6 3

In this case you intend to finesse but have no need for an immediate cover from West. Now the card to play is the ten, for West is not likely to cover this if he has a guarded king. If West does produce the king, therefore, there is a good case for running the seven on the way back.

Some of the old chestnuts are still worth trying.

A 9 4 3

K J 10 8

With no clues to the location of the missing queen, start with the jack from hand. If West does not cover, go up with the ace and run the nine on the way back. West should never cover in this situation, of course, but players sometimes do.

When you are worried about the possibility of an enemy ruff, you may succeed in putting the ace of trumps to sleep for one round by faking a finesse in the trump suit.

K 7 5

Q J 10 6 2

If East is threatening to ruff something, try the effect of playing the jack of trumps from hand. West may play low in the hope that his partner can win with the queen. He will not hold off a second time. but by then East may be out of trumps.

The same ploy can be tried in a side suit when you have a loser too many.

```
              ♠ K 10 4 3
              ♡ J 8 3
              ◇ A Q 4
              ♣ J 6 2
♠ A 8 5                        ♠ 9 7 6 2
♡ K 4                          ♡ A 6
◇ 10 7 5 3                     ◇ J 9 8 2
♣ 10 9 8 3                     ♣ A 5 4
              ♠ Q J
              ♡ Q 10 9 7 5 2
              ◇ K 6
              ♣ K Q 7
```

Both vulnerable.
Dealer South.

South	North
1♡	1♠
2♡	3♡
4♡	Pass

West leads the ten of clubs to his partner's ace and
you win the club continuation with the king. To lead
trumps at this point would be to give up without a
struggle. Instead, try the jack of spades from hand.
West, who cannot yet see four tricks for the defense,
may well play low in the hope of scoring two spades, in
which case your remaining spade loser will go away on
the third diamond and you will lose no more than two
trumps and the ace of clubs.

Although well known, such homely stratagems are
still good for plenty of stolen tricks. Even if West is suspicious, he cannot be sure of what is going on, and you
are bound to get away with it some of the time.

Another type of fake finesse can be highly effective
on certain hands.

```
                    ♠ J 9 3
                    ♡ A 8 7 3
                    ◊ A Q J 4
                    ♣ K 6
♠ K Q 10 6 4                          ♠ 8 7 5
♡ 6                                   ♡ Q J 4
◊ 10 7 5 3                            ◊ 9 2
♣ J 7 4                               ♣ Q 10 9 5 2
                    ♠ A 2
                    ♡ K 10 9 5 2
                    ◊ K 8 6
                    ♣ A 8 3
```

Neither vulnerable.
Dealer North.

West	North	East	South
	1NT	Pass	3♡
Pass	4◊	Pass	6♡
Pass	Pass	Pass	

West attacks your weak spot by leading the king of spades. Winning with the ace, you play off the ace and king of trumps, hoping for a 2-2 split. To your disappointment West shows out on the second round.

Now it looks as though the slam can succeed only if the diamonds are 3-3, but if you handle the suit correctly you can give yourself an extra chance. Play a low diamond for a 'finesse' of the jack, cash the ace and continue with the four of diamonds from the table. If East thinks you are going to ruff he may decline to waste his master trump on a loser. In that case your king will score, and a club to the king will enable you to play the queen of diamonds, discarding your losing spade as the beetroot-faced East ruffs in.

Once again it is worth pointing out that you will not get away with this against defenders who are meticulous about showing their distribution. West will play the seven of diamonds on the first round and complete his echo by dropping the three under dummy's ace. East will therefore know that you have a third diamond, which can only be the king, so he will hasten to ruff and return a spade. Count signals pay their way, as has been mentioned before.

The qualified larcenist is not satisfied with winning the finesses that are right for him. He expects to win some of those that are wrong as well.

A Q 6 4

J 10

Suppose that this is a side suit in a trump contract and the bidding has indicated that East must have the king. There is no reason to despair. Play the jack to dummy's ace and return the four. Many defenders in the East seat will play low, expecting you to ruff. Not, of course, those defenders whose partners have given a count signal.

A 9 5 4

Q 10

A similar ploy can be tried when West leads the jack of this suit. Win with the ace, dropping the queen from your hand, and continue with the four from dummy. The chances of success are better this time since West has had no opportunity to signal.

A pretty variation on this theme is seen in the deal that won the International Bridge Press Association's 'Hand of the Year' award in 1973. This hand, originally written up by Jose le Dentu in *Le Figaro*, was played by Addo Eichel.

```
              ♠ A 8 7
              ♡ Q 5 3
              ◇ A 6 4 3
              ♣ A Q 4
♠ 5 4 2                        ♠ K 6
♡ J                            ♡ K 9 8 7 6 4 2
◇ Q J 8 7                      ◇ 10
♣ J 9 8 3 2                    ♣ K 10 7
              ♠ Q J 10 9 3
              ♡ A 10
              ◇ K 9 5 2
              ♣ 6 5
```

Neither vulnerable.
Dealer North.

West	North	East	South
	1 ◇	3 ♡	3 ♠
Pass	4 ♠	Pass	Pass
Pass			

West led the jack of hearts and declarer paused to
take stock. It would seem natural to cover the jack
with the queen, thus avoiding a heart loser. On the bidding the jack was sure to be a singleton, however, and
Eichel realised that if the spade finesse lost a heart ruff
could prove fatal. He set himself out to persuade East
that West had the ten of hearts by playing low from
dummy and winning with the ace.

When East won the next trick with the king of
spades he shifted, understandably, to the ten of diamonds. South won with the king, drew trumps ending
in dummy, and led the five of hearts from the table.
East confidently played low, but his composure was
shattered when South produced the ten.

Declarer was still not quite out of the wood, for he
had to decide whether to try for his tenth trick in dia-

monds or in clubs. Having done everything right so far, however, he was not about to go wrong now. He cashed his remaining trumps, discarding a club and a diamond from the table, and continued with a diamond to the ace in this position:

```
              ♠  --
              ♡  Q
              ◇  A 6
              ♣  A Q
♠  --                          ♠  --
♡  --                          ♡  K 9 8
◇  Q J 8                       ◇  --
♣  J 9                         ♣  K 10
              ♠  --
              ♡  --
              ◇  9 5 2
              ♣  6 5
```

When East discarded a heart on the ace of diamonds, he was thrown in by the lead of the queen of hearts and had to concede two club tricks at the end.

The declarer was 70 years old when he played this hand, which goes to show that age is no barrier when it comes to trickiness. Older players tend, in fact, to do particularly well in this aspect of the game, having 'been there' so often before.

Chapter 6

LEADING ASTRAY

We are treading on dangerous ground here, for the top priority in choosing an opening lead must be to give partner accurate information about your length and strength in the suit. Nevertheless, there are certain occasions when partner cannot be deceived-- when declarer's length in the suit is known from the bidding, for instance.

	South	North
♠ J 6 5	1NT	2♣
♡ Q J 8 5 2	2♡	2NT
◇ 10 7 4	3NT	Pass
♣ A 3		

The opponents reach three notrump after a Stayman sequence and you have to lead from the above hand. You know (and your partner knows) that South has exactly four cards in hearts (not five or he would have tried three hearts instead of three notrumps). If you decide that a heart lead offers the best chance in spite of the bidding, there is no need to trot out the conventional fourth-highest card. Lead the two instead of the five. Partner won't be fooled but declarer may be.

Opportunities for misdirection are plentiful when your opponents use a highly artificial bidding system. The modern relay systems may reach accurate contracts most of the time, but they often reveal the precise shape of declarer's hand. In such circumstances there is no need to inform partner of your length when you lead or to give any count signals. Select your cards with a view to confusing declarer.

Under normal conditions false-carding on the opening lead is best restricted to those occasions when it cannot matter if partner is deceived.

```
                     ♠ A K 8 6 3
                     ♡ K 7 6 4
                     ◊ 7 5
                     ♣ A K
    ♠ Q 7 2                          ♠ J 10
    ♡ Q 5                            ♡ J 10 8 3
    ◊ A J 8 4 2                      ◊ 10 9 6
    ♣ Q J 5                          ♣ 9 7 6 4
                     ♠ 9 5 4
                     ♡ A 9 2
                     ◊ K Q 3
                     ♣ 10 8 3 2
```

North-South vulnerable.
Dealer West.

West	North	East	South
1 ◊	Double	Pass	1NT
Pass	2NT	Pass	3NT
Pass	Pass	Pass	

Four spades would have been an easier contract, but there is not much wrong with three notrumps which would have been made in comfort on the normal lead of the fourth-highest diamond.

Realising that his partner's actions were not likely to influence the result, however, West decided to inject a little confusion by leading the two of diamonds. The nine drew the king, and at the second trick a spade was played to the ace. When the ten appeared from the East hand, declarer had to consider the possibility that West had started with four spades. Since the diamonds appeared to be 4-4, South decided that he could afford the safety play of a small spade from the table at trick three.

He was swiftly disillusioned. East won the jack of spades and returned the ten of diamonds, and West scored four diamond tricks to put the contract one down.

A good occasion for trying a deceptive lead is when you suspect that a successful finesse will make things easy for declarer.

```
                    ♠ K 7 4
                    ♡ A K J 10 5
                    ◊ 10 7 2
                    ♣ Q 6
    ♠ 10 9 5                       ♠ J 8 6 3
    ♡ Q 9 3                        ♡ 7 6 4
    ◊ A K 9 5 3                    ◊ 8 4
    ♣ A 4                          ♣ 9 7 5 2
                    ♠ A Q 2
                    ♡ 8 2
                    ◊ Q J 6
                    ♣ K J 10 8 3
```

Both vulnerable.
Dealer North.

West	North	East	South
	1 ♡	Pass	2 ♣
Pass	2 ♡	Pass	3NT
Pass	Pass	Pass	

Conditions for deception are ideal here. West knows that his partner cannot have enough in high cards to affect the issue, and the queen of hearts is likely to be well placed for declarer. The three of diamonds almost picks itself as the opening lead.

After winning the first trick declarer has to decide

whether he is going to rely on the heart finesse for his contract or risk knocking out the ace of clubs. Believing West to have led from a four-card suit, he is likely to adopt the latter course and go down.

Had the five of diamonds been led, declarer might well have decided that the heart finesse represented the best chance of making his contract.

It can sometimes be profitable to foster the illusion that you have led from a five-card suit.

```
            ♠  10 4
            ♡  K 9 4 3
            ◇  Q 10 6
            ♣  Q 8 7 2
♠ K 7 2                     ♠  8 6 5 3
♡ A 10                      ♡  J 8 6 5
◇ A 9 5 3                   ◇  8 7 4
♣ J 9 6 4                   ♣  10 3
            ♠  A Q J 9
            ♡  Q 7 2
            ◇  K J 2
            ♣  A K 5
```

North-South vulnerable.
Dealer West.

West	North	East	South
1 ◇	Pass	Pass	Double
Pass	1 ♡	Pass	2NT
Pass	3NT	Pass	Pass
Pass			

Partner is not likely to be able to contribute much to the defense, so you decide to lead the five of diamonds, not with any specific purpose in mind but just to stir things up a little. Declarer wins in dummy and runs the ten of spades to your king. Now you can see how the deception may work to your advantage and you follow up with the three of diamonds.

If declarer is convinced that you began with five cards in diamonds he will not dare to try for his ninth trick in hearts, since you are marked with the ace. After cashing his spades, on which you discard the ten of hearts, South will play three rounds of clubs hoping for a 3-3 break. As it happens, this establishes a fifth trick for the defense.

A defender occasionally has the chance to play a telling false card on the second round of a suit. The next hand comes from a team game.

```
              ♠  A J 5
              ♡  Q J 10 6
              ◊  10 9 3
              ♣  J 9 4
♠  10 7 2                      ♠  9 8 6 3
♡  A 9 3                       ♡  8 5 4 2
◊  8 4                         ◊  Q 7 2
♣  K 8 6 3 2                   ♣  A 5
              ♠  K Q 4
              ♡  K 7
              ◊  A K J 6 5
              ♣  Q 10 7
```

Both vulnerable.
Dealer South.

South	North
1 ◊	1 ♡
2NT	3NT

The contract was the same in both rooms, as was the opening lead of the three of clubs. East won the first trick with the ace and returned the five of clubs. In one room West took his king and played a third round of clubs to clear the suit. On this defense, however, it was clear to declarer that the contract was in danger if

West regained the lead. Faced with a choice of plays, he eventually did the right thing by cashing one top diamond, entering dummy in spades and finessing against the queen of diamonds. Five diamonds, three spades and a club added up to nine tricks.

In the other room West calmly followed with the six of clubs on the second round. This gave declarer the impression that the clubs were divided 4-3, in which case nine safe tricks could be made by knocking out the ace of hearts. Great was his disappointment when West took the heart ace and cashed three more clubs to defeat the contract.

Enough swings can be created by quiet deceptive moves like this to decide the result of any match. The most attractive and difficult swindles of this type are those in which both defenders have a part to play.

		♠ A 6	
		♡ J 8 4	
		◊ Q 6 5	
♠ K 10 8 5 4		♣ A J 10 3 2	♠ Q 9 2
♡ 9 6 3			♡ A 10 7 2
◊ 10 2			◊ 8 4 3
♣ K 9 5		♠ J 7 3	♣ 7 6 4
		♡ K Q 5	
		◊ A K J 9 7	
		♣ Q 8	

Both vulnerable.
Dealer South.

South	North
1NT	3NT

At both tables in a match the five of spades was led and the queen won the first trick. One of the East players made the normal return of the nine of spades to dummy's ace. It was clear that the spades were breaking 5-3, and the declarer realised that he could not afford to knock out the ace of hearts. Accordingly he entered his hand with a diamond and tried the club finesse. With the clubs behaving kindly he had no trouble in taking eleven tricks.

At the other table East, aware of the menace of dummy's clubs, tried the effect of returning the two of spades. West was deceived into thinking that his partner had a doubleton, but he reasoned that it could not cost to follow with the eight on the second round, concealing the four.

This card fitted perfectly into the false picture that East was promoting. It appeared to declarer that the spades were 4-4, in which case there was no need to hazard the club finesse. South therefore led a heart at trick three, but East hopped up with the ace and produced the nine of spades. Surprised but gratified, West took three more tricks in the suit.

Opportunities for a deceptive return at trick two are quite frequent. Consider this ordinary hand.

```
                      ♠ Q 3
                      ♡ Q 9 5
                      ◇ A J 10 9 4
    ♠ J 8 7 4         ♣ A 7 5         ♠ A 10 5 2
    ♡ 10 7 4 3                        ♡ 8 6 2
    ◇ 7 5 3                           ◇ K 6
    ♣ 4 2                             ♣ K Q J 3
                      ♠ K 9 6
                      ♡ A K J
                      ◇ Q 8 2
                      ♣ 10 9 8 6
```

Both vulnerable.
Dealer South.

South	West	North	East
1♣	Pass	1◇	Pass
1NT	Pass	3NT	Pass
Pass	Pass		

West leads the four of spades to the queen, ace and six. Looking at that strong dummy, East can see that he can hope for little help from partner. The jack of spades is about the only significant card that West can have, which means that only three spade tricks can be established--not enough to set the contract. If East returns the two of spades, declarer will go up with the queen, take the losing finesse in diamonds, and eventually score nine tricks.

An immediate club shift is unlikely to fare better since South is marked with four cards in the suit, although a shift to the club three has the small technical chance of finding partner with a doubleton ten.

By far the best chance is a psychological one. At trick two East should return the ten of spades, playing on declarer's fears of a 5-3 break. South is virtually certain to hold up the king. He will realise that he has been swindled when West follows with the seven, but it will be too late. With two spade tricks in the bag, East can shift to the king of clubs, developing the setting tricks in that suit.

In the pairs game there is an art in turning declarer's greed for overtricks to your advantage.

```
                    ♠ Q 5
                    ♡ A 8 3
                    ◇ K 8
                    ♣ K J 10 7 6 2
   ♠ 7 6 3                         ♠ J 10 8 2
   ♡ Q J 10 7                      ♡ K 6 2
   ◇ 10 6 4 3                      ◇ 9 5 2
   ♣ 8 4                           ♣ A 9 3
                    ♠ A K 9 4
                    ♡ 9 5 4
                    ◇ A Q J 7
                    ♣ Q 5
```

Match-point pairs.
Neither vulnerable.
Dealer South.

South	North
South	*North*
1NT	3NT

West leads the queen of hearts and a depressing dummy goes down. East can see that declarer must have just about every missing face-card outside the heart suit, and it is clear that this contract is not going to be defeated.

Declarer plays low from dummy to the first trick. If East also plays low, declarer will keep dummy's ace of hearts for the third round and will subsequently make ten tricks. What East should do, of course, is overtake the queen of hearts with his king and return the suit. South may then see no reason to hold up the ace of hearts on the second round. On a 5-2 heart split he must go down if West has the ace of clubs, but he will expect to make eleven tricks when East has it. In trying for eleven tricks he will succeed in holding himself to nine.

We see the other side of the coin if one of East's small hearts is traded for one of West's diamonds. Now East can steal an extra trick for the defense by playing low at trick one instead of overtaking. Declarer will hold up the ace again, thus limiting himself to ten tricks.

Trump Protection

A defender with potential but uncertain trump tricks should give some thought to the best way of protecting his holding. The slam swing that developed on this hand from a team game highlights an aspect of the opening lead that is largely neglected in the textbooks.

```
                    ♠ A K Q 7 4 2
                    ♡ K J
                    ◊ K J 7 3
                    ♣ 6
  ♠ J 5                              ♠ 10 9 6 3
  ♡ 9 4                              ♡ Q 10 7 6 5 2
  ◊ A 10 8 4                         ◊ --
  ♣ Q 10 7 4 2                       ♣ 9 5 3
                    ♠ 8
                    ♡ A 8 3
                    ◊ Q 9 6 5 2
                    ♣ A K J 8
```

Neither vulnerable.
Dealer South.

South	North
1 ◊	2 ♣
3 ♣	3 ◊
3 ♡	3 ♠
4 ♣	5NT
6 ◊	Pass

The diamond slam was reached in both rooms on similar bidding. At one table the opening lead was the nine of hearts, which was covered by the jack, queen and ace. The declarer saw that the slam was in no danger unless the trumps were 4-0. He could cope with a void in either hand, but he had to make up his mind immediately about the most likely location of the void and the only clue lay in the opening lead. West appeared to be short in hearts and might therefore have long diamonds. Accordingly South played the queen of diamonds from hand at trick two, and this proved to be the right move. West won and returned a heart to the king, but after ruffing a spade in hand South was able to finesse twice against West's remaining trumps to bring home the slam.

At the other table West chose to lead the four of clubs, which gave the declarer a completely different picture of the hand. If West had length in clubs it seemed unlikely that he would also be long in trumps. South therefore played a low diamond to the jack at trick two and was subsequently unable to avoid the loss of two trumps.

The lesson is plain. A defender with potential trump tricks who has to lead against a slam will have the best chance of scoring his trumps if he leads from length, or at least gives the appearance of leading from length.

Conversely, a defender who is short in trumps should try to protect his partner's holding by leading from shortage, or appearing to lead from shortage. If East had to lead against six diamonds by North on the last hand, the nine of clubs would be a good choice.

Underhand Play

Opportunities for deception abound when a defender leads through dummy's known strength, either on the opening lead or later in the play.

When you know that the trumps are breaking badly for declarer, it is often a good idea to attack one of his options on the opening lead.

Both vulnerable.
Dealer North.

		North	South
♠	J 10 6 4	1♡	1♠
♡	K 8 3	3◇	3♠
◇	6	4♠	6♠
♣	Q J 7 5 4		

You have to find a lead from the above West hand, and the prospects are mixed. You have a surprise for declarer in trumps, and the diamonds appear to be breaking badly for him. The unfavorable factor is the presence of the king of hearts in your hand, where it is probably well placed for declarer.

Once South learns that he has a trump loser, he may be able to recover by taking the heart finesse. But if you put him under immediate pressure by leading the eight of hearts, he may reject the heart finesse and subsequently regret it. The full deal could be:

```
                    ♠ A 5
                    ♡ A Q J 9 4
                    ◇ A K 10 8 3
                    ♣ 3
♠ J 10 6 4                          ♠ 2
♡ K 8 3                             ♡ 10 7 6
◇ 6                                 ◇ J 9 5 4 2
♣ Q J 7 5 4                         ♣ 10 8 6 2
                    ♠ K Q 9 8 7 3
                    ♡ 5 2
                    ◇ Q 7
                    ♣ A K 9
```

Would you finesse in hearts at trick one? Of course not. You would go up with the ace, ruff your losing club with dummy's small spade, cash the spade ace, enter hand with the queen of diamonds and attempt to draw the remaining trumps. In the event of a 4-1 trump break you would expect to be able to discard the losing heart on the third round of diamonds. Unlucky!

It is rare for a first-class defender to underlead an ace against a trump contract, so when the maneuver *is* attempted it can have a devastating effect. On the following hand both defenders contributed to declarer's downfall.

```
                    ♠ K 10 6
                    ♡ K Q 10 8
                    ◊ A 7 3
♠ A 5 3             ♣ K Q 3             ♠ Q J 8 2
♡ J 9 6                                 ♡ A 7 4 2
◊ J 8 5                                 ◊ Q 6
♣ A J 8 4           ♠ 9 7 4             ♣ 10 9 5
                    ♡ 5 3
                    ◊ K 10 9 4 2
                    ♣ 7 6 2
```

Neither vulnerable.
Dealer West.

West	North	East	South
Pass	1 ♡	Pass	Pass
1NT	Double	Pass	2 ◊
Pass	Pass	Pass	

No lead was particularly attractive and West made the happy choice of the three of spades. The declarer played low from dummy and East gave no sign of surprise when his jack won the trick. East returned the ten of clubs and dummy's queen was allowed to win.

After cashing the ace and king of diamonds, South played a heart to dummy's queen on which East calmly played the two. South's next move was to concede the third round of trumps to the jack.

West produced the five of spades with the proper degree of unconcern, and declarer can hardly be blamed for going wrong. It appeared to South that West had the ace of clubs and hearts plus the jack of diamonds. Since he had passed originally, West could not hold the ace of spades as well although there was room for him to have the queen. South therefore played the ten of spades from dummy, and the defenders took six tricks to beat the unbeatable contract.

Here is another occasion for underleading an ace.

```
          K 8 7 6
A Q J 9                      5 3 2
          10 4
```

If North has bid the suit, a lead of the queen will sometimes produce a second trick for the defense. Declarer will not play low from dummy if he has a singleton in the suit, of course, so West must choose his moment carefully.

Underleading the king and queen can be effective when the ace and the jack are in dummy.

```
          A J 5
K Q 6 3                      10 8 4
          9 7 2
```

The lead of a low card by West will produce a second trick for the defense more often than not.

```
          J 9 3
K Q 7 4                      10 6 2
          A 8 5
```

This is the same thing in a different form. When West leads the four declarer is likely to play low from the table. To put up the jack is against the odds.

A variation of this coup made an appearance some years ago in an open pairs at the American Spring Nationals.

```
                    ♠ 6
                    ♡ Q 10 9 6
                    ◇ J 9 5 3
                    ♣ 9 8 6 5
♠ A 9 5 3                              ♠ Q 10 8 7
♡ A                                    ♡ J 5 3 2
◇ K Q 8 4 2                            ◇ 10 7
♣ A J 7                                ♣ 10 4 3
                    ♠ K J 4 2
                    ♡ K 8 7 4
                    ◇ A 6
                    ♣ K Q 2
```

Match-point pairs.

North-South vulnerable.

Dealer South.

South	West	North	East
1NT	Pass	Pass	Pass

West took the view that he was too strong to double, and one notrump became the final contract. The lead of the four of diamonds was covered by the nine and ten. South won the trick and played a small heart to knock out the ace. At this point Jim Mathis in the West seat found the sadistic continuation of the eight of diamonds!

Well, what would you have done? South naturally played low from dummy, hoping that East had started with K 10 or Q 10 doubleton in which case the suit would be blocked. A moment later his cheeks were burning as West produced the three remaining diamonds. South discarded two spades and a club from hand, and West continued with the ace and another club to ensure a two-trick defeat.

In practice the declarer decided that he did not wish to see minus 200 entered against his name. After playing a heart to the queen and running the ten of hearts, he tried to steal back a trick by playing a spade to his king. That made it minus 300.

If underleading the king and queen is not exciting enough, you can always try underleading the king, queen and jack. The next deal features Tim Seres of Australia, one of the top players in the world and one of the great masters of deception. Of course, Seres came originally from Hungary where trickiness is a national characteristic. No offense to my many good friends in Hungary is intended when I mention that Hungarians have been described as the sort of people who can follow you into a revolving door and come out ahead of you.

Anyway, here is Tim Seres coming out ahead of his opponents in the 1971 Bermuda Bowl.

```
                    ♠ J
                    ♡ Q 8 7 4
                    ◊ K Q 10 3
                    ♣ A 10 8 5
♠ K 8 4 2                           ♠ 10 6 5 2
♡ 9 3                               ♡ K 6 5 2
◊ A 7                               ◊ J 9 5
♣ K Q J 7 2                         ♣ 9 6
                    ♠ A Q 9 7
                    ♡ A J 10
                    ◊ 8 6 4 2
                    ♣ 4 3
```

East-West vulnerable.
Dealer South.

South	West	North	East
Mathe	Seres	Krauss	Cummings
1♠	Pass	2♣	Pass
2◊	Pass	2♡	Pass
2NT	Pass	3◊	Pass
3NT	Pass	Pass	Pass

It is a very tight game but, with the favourable lie of the cards in the red suits, it looked like being a good board for North America.

Seres had different ideas. He settled the issue at trick one by producing the devastating lead of the two of clubs. Mathe naturally tried the eight from dummy and Cummings, on winning with the nine, was not slow to return the suit.

In the other room the Australians made 140 in three hearts for a gain of 5 i.m.p. on the board.

Just about the cheekiest underlead of all time was

made by Pietro Bernasconi of Switzerland playing against France in the 1976 Team Olympiad.

```
              ♠ K Q 9
              ♡ A J 6 5 2
              ◇ K J
              ♣ A 9 7
♠ 8 4 2                        ♠ 10 7 5 3
♡ K Q 10 9 7 4                 ♡ 8 3
◇ A Q 4                        ◇ 8 5 3
♣ 10                           ♣ Q 8 5 2
              ♠ A J 6
              ♡ --
              ◇ 10 9 7 6 2
              ♣ K J 6 4 3
```

East-West vulnerable.
Dealer North.

West	North	East	South
	1♡	Pass	1NT
Pass	3NT	Pass	Pass
Pass			

The contract was the same in both rooms, and the Swiss declarer had no difficulty in making ten tricks after the opening lead of the king of hearts.

In the other room Bernasconi produced the more imaginative lead of the ten of hearts. Declarer did not like this attack one little bit. He played low from dummy, discarding a diamond from hand, and low again on the continuation of the nine of hearts, this time discarding a spade.

West continued fiendishly with the seven of hearts and South went up with the ace, only to realise how thoroughly he had been tricked when East discarded a diamond. Throwing another diamond himself, South cashed the ace of clubs and ran the nine of clubs when East played low on the next round. He was thus able to scramble home with five clubs, three spades and a heart.

The gain to Switzerland was only 1 i.m.p., but Bernasconi's defense deserved a larger reward. Consider what would have happened if East had covered the nine of clubs with his queen. The club suit would then have been blocked by dummy's seven. Because of the declarer's earlier discard of a spade, he would have been unable to establish the club suit without abandoning one of the spades in dummy and the contract would have gone one down.

Chapter 7

THE CAMOUFLAGE NET

An important attribute of the tricky declarer is his skill in the art of camouflage. Your constant aim should be to conceal your distribution and the location of your high cards from the defenders until the play is well advanced. The longer you can keep the enemy in the dark about your holdings the better will be your chance of making an impossible contract. For this reason good players often depart from the text-book method of handling certain suit combinations.

K J 7 6 4

9 3   Q 10 8

A 5 2

If you need four tricks from this suit it is technically correct to start with the ace, catering for the possibility of a singleton queen in the East hand. But for deceptive purposes it will usually work out better if you start with a low card from hand, concealing the presence of your ace. When the finesse of the jack loses to the queen, East may not realise that the rest of the suit is yours to run.

Q 7 4

J 3   A 10 5

K 9 8 6 2

Suppose you play a low card to the queen, losing to the ace. When you regain the lead you should continue with a low card from hand. Each opponent may then believe that his partner has the king, and this may affect the subsequent defense.

If you have a weakness elsewhere in the hand, it can pay to concede an early trick in a suit even when there is some possibility of running the suit without loss.

```
                    ♠ 9 6 5
                    ♡ Q 8 3
                    ◊ A 9 7 4 3
                    ♣ A 9
♠ 10 8 7 4 2                        ♠ Q 3
♡ A 10 4                            ♡ K J 9 2
◊ 10 6 2                            ◊ Q J 5
♣ 7 3                              ♣ J 10 5 4
                    ♠ A K J
                    ♡ 7 6 5
                    ◊ K 8
                    ♣ K Q 8 6 2
```

Both vulnerable.
Dealer South.

South	North
1NT	3NT

In a match the bidding was the same at both tables, as was the opening lead of the four of spades. Capturing the queen with his king, one declarer played the clubs from the top, conceding the fourth round to East. West, however, had the opportunity to discard one spade and the ten of hearts, so it was not difficult for East to find the deadly heart shift.

The other declarer, noting that he needed only four club tricks, played a club to dummy's nine at trick two. Now it was hard for East, without the benefit of a signal from his partner, to work out what was going on. After winning the ten of clubs East returned his second spade and the hand was over.

When a trick has to be lost in the process of developing a suit it is best conceded at the earliest possible moment.

8 7 5 3 2

Q 10   J 6 4

A K 9

Start this suit with a 'finesse' of the nine, and again the defenders may not realise that they have no further stopper.

At pairs, where overtricks are the spice of life, it is particularly important to conceal your assets.

♠ Q 5
♡ 7 3
◊ A 8 6 5 4 2
♣ K Q 4

♠ A 9 2	♠ K 10 7 4 3
♡ K 10 9 8 4 2	♡ J 6
◊ Q 10 9	◊ J 6
♣ 7	♣ J 9 5 2

♠ J 8 6
♡ A Q 5
◊ K 3
♣ A 10 8 6 3

Match-point pairs.

Neither vulnerable.
Dealer South.

South	West	North	East
1♣	1♡	2◊	Pass
2NT	Pass	3NT	Pass
Pass	Pass		

West leads the ten of hearts to the jack and queen. South can see that he is fairly safe for nine tricks since West is not likely to have length in clubs. The only possible source of overtricks is the diamond suit, and South should direct his efforts toward developing the diamonds without giving too much away to the opponents.

The right move is to play the three of diamonds from hand and duck in dummy. The defender who wins this trick is likely to return a heart, feeling that time is on his side. He will soon discover that appearances are deceptive, for the heart return gives South twelve tricks and a top score.

Declarer would have made no more than ten tricks if he had cashed the top diamonds before conceding the loser. East would have the chance to encourage in spades, but even without this aid West would surely see the urgent need to cash out.

When the defenders attack your weak spot, you can sometimes arrange a stay of execution until you have stolen your ninth trick in notrumps.

```
                    ♠ 7 2
                    ♡ Q 7 6
                    ◊ 9 5 3
                    ♣ Q J 10 8 5
  ♠ A 10 8 6 3                       ♠ Q 9 4
  ♡ J 8 4 2                          ♡ A 9 3
  ◊ J 7                              ◊ Q 10 8 6 2
  ♣ 6 3                              ♣ 4 2
                    ♠ K J 5
                    ♡ K 10 5
                    ◊ A K 4
                    ♣ A K 9 7
```

Both vulnerable.
Dealer South.

South	North
2NT	3NT

West leads the six of spades to the queen and king. You have only eight immediate winners and have to try for the ninth trick in hearts. There is no danger if the spades are 4-4 or if West has the ace of hearts, but if East has the heart ace a spade return could spoil your score card.

However, you can give yourself an extra chance when the clubs are 2-2. Play off the ace and king of clubs, and then table the king of hearts. If East believes you are trying to gain entry to the clubs with the queen of hearts he may hold up his ace, in which case you can run for home in the minors.

East should not be blamed too much for getting it wrong. After all, he cannot be sure that the spades are his to run, and his partner's echo in clubs could indicate four cards in the suit.

Fortunately the defenders are unable to see through the backs of the cards, and by taking advantage of this you can steal the odd trick or two.

J 7 4

K 10 8 2   A 9 3

Q 6 5

There is no genuine chance of a trick if you have to tackle this suit yourself. The best you can do is try a lead of the jack from dummy. Who knows? Perhaps East will play low in the hope that his partner will win with the queen. West has to win with the king, in fact, and a further lead from dummy sets up a trick for your queen.

The most hopeless holdings sometimes yield tricks in a surprising way.

K 7 5

A 9 3   Q 10 7 2

J 8 4

If you are in dummy and need a fast trick from this suit, try leading the king. It is not unknown for a defender to hold off in the West position. What is more, if you have the brass neck to continue with a small card to the jack, West may hold off again, placing you with queen, jack and others.

The play of an unsupported king from the closed hand can also be surprisingly effective on occasion. Here is a hand from a European Championship match between Great Britain and Sweden many years ago.

```
                    ♠ 6 4
                    ♡ 7 3
                    ◇ 8 5 3 2
                    ♣ J 9 7 4 3
  ♠ 9 7 3                              ♠ J 10 8 5
  ♡ Q J 10 8 4                         ♡ 9 6 5 2
  ◇ 9 6                                ◇ A 7 4
  ♣ A 10 8                             ♣ Q 6
                    ♠ A K Q 2
                    ♡ A K
                    ◇ K Q J 10
                    ♣ K 5 2
```

Both vulnerable.
Dealer South.

South	West	North	East
Wohlin	Reese	Jannersten	Schapiro
2♣	Pass	2◇	Pass
2♠	Pass	3♣	Pass
3NT	Pass	Pass	Pass

The lead of the queen of hearts attacked the weak spot immediately, and Wohlin saw that he would make no more than eight tricks if he knocked out the ace of diamonds. Undaunted, he won the first trick and played the king of clubs from hand. Reese naturally held up the ace since South might well have had K Q x in clubs. With a club trick in the bag, Wohlin played on diamonds to set up his nine tricks.

It is worth noting that apart from the deceptive angle Wohlin's play had a small genuine chance of success. If East had held the queen of clubs singleton, there would have been no way for the defenders to beat the contract after the king of clubs at trick two.

Another way of deflecting a dangerous enemy attack is by use of the pseudo hold-up.

J 10 5   Q 10 3

A 4   A 2

Suppose that in these two positions West leads the nine against your notrump contract. There is a danger that the entire suit will be run against you if you win the first round. Unless you can be sure of keeping West out of the lead, the best shot in each case is to play the ten from dummy and duck in hand when East covers. Ignorant of the true position, East is likely to shift, waiting for his partner to lead the suit again.

This hand shows an allied position.

```
                        ♠ K 6 4
                        ♡ Q 10 3
                        ◇ A Q J 6 5 2
                        ♣ 6
      ♠ A 7                               ♠ 10 9 5 3
      ♡ 8 7 2                             ♡ A J 9 6 4
      ◇ K 8 4                             ◇ 3
      ♣ K Q 9 7 2                         ♣ 8 5 4
                        ♠ Q J 8 2
                        ♡ K 5
                        ◇ 10 9 7
                        ♣ A J 10 3
```

Both vulnerable.
Dealer West.

West	North	East	South
1 ♣	1 ◊	1 ♡	2NT
Pass	3NT	Pass	Pass
Pass			

West leads the eight of hearts. How do you like your chances? You don't like them at all, of course. You have only one heart stopper and, although the diamond finesse is sure to be right, there are no more than eight legitimate tricks. If you play low from dummy at trick one East will let you have the trick, and when West comes in with the ace of spades he will play another heart to give his partner four tricks in the suit. West is not likely to let you slip the jack of spades past his ace in this situation.

However, East cannot know at this stage how many hearts his partner has. You can take advantage of this by playing just as though you had three hearts and West two. Put up the queen of hearts at trick one. East will not dare to duck for fear of allowing you to make a second trick in the suit. For same reason he will not continue hearts but shift to a club, and that is all the help you need. Up with the ace of clubs and finesse in diamonds. After a couple of rounds of diamonds you can knock out the ace of spades, and the defenders will be able to take no more than one spade, one heart and two clubs.

At times you need to enlist the help of the defenders to avoid a guess in the trump suit.

```
              ♠ K
              ♡ Q 9 3
              ◇ A J 7 6 2
              ♣ A 9 8 3
♠ 9 8 5 2                      ♠ A 10 7 6 4
♡ K J 5                       ♡ 2
◇ 9 5                         ◇ Q 10 8 3
♣ K Q 10 4                    ♣ J 7 2
              ♠ Q J 3
              ♡ A 10 8 7 6 4
              ◇ K 4
              ♣ 6 5
```

East-West vulnerable.
Dealer North.

West	North	East	South
	1 ◇	Pass	1 ♡
Pass	2 ♣	Pass	2 ♡
Pass	4 ♡	Pass	Pass
Pass			

West leads the king of clubs to dummy's ace. There is just one loser in each of the black suits, and you can see that the contract will be made if you can avoid the loss of two trumps. How do you play the trumps?

You don't play trumps, of course, for there is a good chance that you can persuade the defenders to do it for you. The first move is to play the king of spades from dummy.

Winning with the ace, East has no way of telling that you have no more spade losers. He is quite likely to return his trump with a view to cutting down ruffs in dummy. And that gives you ten tricks without the headache of guessing the trump position.

The secret of bringing home impossible contracts is to make it as hard as possible for the defenders to do the right thing. One maneuver that is practically guaranteed to succeed is the 'Chinese finesse.'

```
                    ♠ A 10 7 4
                    ♡ A
                    ◊ K 10 9 6 3
                    ♣ K 6 5
♠ K 9                                   ♠ Q 8 5 2
♡ Q 10 9 6 4 3                          ♡ 8 7 5
◊ A 7 4                                 ◊ Q 5
♣ 9 4                                   ♣ J 10 7 2
                    ♠ J 6 3
                    ♡ K J 2
                    ◊ J 8 2
                    ♣ A Q 8 3
```

Both vulnerable.
Dealer South.

South	West	North	East
1♣	1♡	2◊	Pass
2NT	Pass	3NT	Pass
Pass	Pass		

West leads the ten of hearts to dummy's ace. Needing to set up the diamonds, an unimaginative declarer might come to hand with a club and run the diamond eight. East would win and clear the hearts and the contract would go two down.

Declarer should realise that he can afford to lose two diamonds on this hand provided that the first one is lost to West, who cannot profitably lead another heart. If the diamond finesse is working, in fact, there is no need to take it. What do you think will happen if declarer plays a small diamond from dummy at trick two? Will East hop up with the queen and return a heart? Not on your life! East has no way of knowing what is going on, and even an expert defender is likely to play low without a quiver, hoping to score his queen on the second round. Whether West takes his ace or not, you will naturally play the king on the second round, making your contract with two overtricks.

Placing the lead was the real theme of the last hand, although it had deceptive overtones. The next example is similar.

```
              ♠ Q J 5
              ♡ K 6
              ◇ A Q J 2
              ♣ K 10 5 3
♠ K 7 4                        ♠ 3
♡ 9 8 2                        ♡ Q J 10 7 5 4
◇ 9 6 4                        ◇ K 7 5
♣ J 9 7 2                      ♣ A Q 8
              ♠ A 10 9 8 6 2
              ♡ A 3
              ◇ 10 8 3
              ♣ 6 4
```

Both vulnerable.
Dealer East.

West	North	East	South
		1♡	1♠
Pass	4♠	Pass	Pass
Pass			

West leads the eight of hearts against your spade game. It looks natural to win with the king and run the queen of spades, but the natural thing is not always right. In this case you know that East will have most of the high cards but there is room for West to have one of them. If West has the ace of clubs or the king of diamonds, your contract is in no danger. You are at risk only when West's honor is the king of spades.

Once again, if the key finesse is right there is no need

to take it. You should therefore win the first trick in hand and play a low spade towards dummy's queen. You don't mind if East produces the king, for the defense will make no more than three tricks. Meanwhile you have the extra chance that if West has the king he will play low, fearing to collide with a singleton ace in his partner's hand. If the queen of spades wins you will draw a second round with the ace and then run the ten of diamonds. Eventually one of your losing clubs will go away on the fourth diamond as West ruffs with his master trump.

On some hands it is quickly apparent that there is no genuine play for the contract. There may still be a psychological chance, but only if you can keep the opponents in the dark about the position of your key cards and the extent of your problems.

```
                    ♠ 7
                    ♡ A 10 8
                    ◇ Q 10 9 6 3
                    ♣ K Q J 5
  ♠ A K 10 4 2                        ♠ J 9 8 3
  ♡ Q 7 2                             ♡ 9 4 3
  ◇ A 8 5                             ◇ K 4
  ♣ 9 4                               ♣ 10 8 3 2
                    ♠ Q 6 5
                    ♡ K J 6 5
                    ◇ J 7 2
                    ♣ A 7 6
```

North-South vulnerable.
Dealer West.

West	North	East	South
1♠	Double	3♠	Double
Pass	4◇	Pass	4♡
Pass	Pass	Pass	

West led the king of spades and continued with the ace, which was ruffed in dummy. From the bidding and the play it was clear that the diamond honors would be divided and that West would have the heart queen. There was no conceivable way of making the contract unless the help of the defenders could be enlisted, so South tried the effect of playing the ten of diamonds from dummy at trick three.

With all four hands exposed it is easy to see that East should play the king. If the defenders play three rounds of diamonds and then shift to clubs, the contract must go two down. But in practice it was not quite so easy. It seemed to East that declarer wanted him to cover the ten of diamonds, so he decided to do the other thing. West won with the ace and could have saved the day by continuing the suit. After two diamonds and a club shift the contract is still one down. But West tried to force dummy again with a third spade. This gave declarer the extra entry he needed to finesse the ten of hearts, draw trumps and claim ten tricks.

A simple way of exploiting the ignorance of a defender is to force him to make an early discard or two. Watch Eric Murray of Canada at work in the 1980 Team Olympiad.

```
                  ♠ K Q 5
                  ♡ K Q 8 7 2
                  ◊ K 2
                  ♣ A Q 4
 ♠ J 8 3 2                          ♠ 9 7 6
 ♡ J 10 9 3                         ♡ 4
 ◊ 10 7                             ◊ J 9 8 6 4
 ♣ 6 5 2                            ♣ J 10 7 3
                  ♠ A 10 4
                  ♡ A 6 5
                  ◊ A Q 5 3
                  ♣ K 9 8
```

East-West vulnerable.
Dealer East.

West	North Kehela	East	South Murray
		Pass	1NT
Pass	2 ◊	Pass	2NT
Pass	3 ♡	Pass	3 ♠
Pass	4NT	Pass	5 ♠
Pass	5NT	Pass	6 ◊
Pass	7NT	Pass	Pass
Pass			

In the match between Canada and Israel, Murray and Kehela bid smoothly to the grand slam. West led the six of clubs to the four, ten and king.

There were twelve top tricks and the thirteenth trick would come from hearts if the suit behaved reasonably. Murray cashed the ace of hearts and played a second heart to the king, receiving the bad news when East discarded a spade. Now the prospects were distinctly poor, for West was not likely to have length in both red suits and there was no other possible squeeze.

However, Murray realised that East might feel himself under pressure if he had length in both minors. Accordingly he played three rounds of spades, the suit in which he was known from the bidding to have no more than three cards, and then played the queen of hearts.

East was able to discard a diamond on the third round of spades, but when the queen of hearts was played he had to make a decision about which minor to keep. There were no clues from the bidding or from his partner's lead, which could have been from either two or three cards. Eventually East guessed wrong by discarding another diamond, and the 'impossible' grand slam was made for a swing of 17 i.m.p. to Canada.

Chapter 8

MENACING TRUMPS

There are many ways in which the defenders can enlist the power of the trump suit on their side. This naturally has to be done in the early stages of the play before declarer has had the opportunity of drawing trumps. Often it is possible to create a losing option for declarer out of thin air.

Q 10 7 5

A K 3   J 8 2

9 6 4

Suppose that declarer is playing in a trump contract and that this is one of the side suits. West leads the king and East encourages with the eight. Thinking that his partner will be able to ruff the third round, West continues with the ace and another. East completes his echo on the second round, and declarer is also convinced that East is going to ruff. It is highly likely that South will play the ten from dummy on the third round, allowing East to score a trick with his jack.

Fear of a ruff is one of the strongest motivations of declarer's play and should be duly exploited by the defense. A declarer can be tortured by a false echo in situations like the following.

```
                    ♠ 6 3
                    ♡ A K J 7 4 2
                    ◇ A J 8 4
                    ♣ 6
♠ A K Q 10 7                              ♠ 9 4 2
♡ 9 8 3                                   ♡ Q 10 5
◇ --                                      ◇ 10 9 7 2
♣ J 9 7 4 3                               ♣ Q 8 2
                    ♠ J 8 5
                    ♡ 6
                    ◇ K Q 6 5 3
                    ♣ A K 10 5
```

Both vulnerable.
Dealer South.

South	West	North	East
1◇	1♠	2♡	Pass
3♣	Pass	4◇	Pass
5◇	Pass	Pass	Pass

West began with top spades and East, seeing no chance of a third trick for the defense outside the trump suit, echoed with the nine and the two. Although aware of the possibility of deception on East's part, declarer could not be sure what was the right thing to do. Since a 6-2 spade break seemed a more real threat than a 4-0 division in trumps, South eventually decided to take East's cards at face value by ruffing the third round of spades with the jack of diamonds.

When East followed with the four of spades on the third round declarer suspected that he had been conned, but it was too late to do anything about it. There was now no way of denying East a trump trick and the unbeatable contract was beaten.

There are many variations on this theme of threat ening a third-round ruff. Here is an attractive one.

```
                    ♠ A Q 10 3
                    ♡ 9 8
                    ◇ K Q 9 5
                    ♣ 10 7 2
♠ 5                                    ♠ J 9 4
♡ K Q 10 6 5                           ♡ A 7 2
◇ 8 6 4 3 2                            ◇ 7
♣ 5 3                                  ♣ A Q J 9 6 4
                    ♠ K 8 7 6 2
                    ♡ J 4 3
                    ◇ A J 10
                    ♣ K 8
```

North-South vulnerable.
Dealer East.

West	North	East	South
		1♣	Double
1♡	2♡	Double	2♠
Pass	4♠	Pass	Pass
Pass			

Looking at all four hands it is hard to see how the contract can go down, for the defenders have no more than two tricks in hearts and one in clubs.

But East was a player who believed in giving declarers every chance to go wrong. When West led the king of hearts East overtook with the ace, cashed the ace of clubs, and returned the two of hearts to his partner's ten. West continued with the queen of hearts, and the declarer was on the familiar guessing griddle.

From the play it seemed likely that East had only two hearts and would over-ruff dummy if given the chance. Rather than risk ruffing with the ten of spades, South ruffed with the queen, hoping to find a 2-2 trump division or a singleton jack. He was soon disillusioned and another ironclad contract hit the dust.

There are some clever ways of persuading a declarer that it would be too dangerous to finesse in trumps. A chance was missed on the following hand.

```
                 ♠ 7
                 ♡ A K J 10 5
                 ◊ A K
                 ♣ Q 8 6 5 2
♠ Q 10 6 4 3                      ♠ K 9 5 2
♡ 9 8 7                           ♡ Q 6 2
◊ J 9 7 6 2                       ◊ 10 5 4
♣ --                             ♣ K J 3
                 ♠ A J 8
                 ♡ 4 3
                 ◊ Q 8 3
                 ♣ A 10 9 7 4
```

North South vulnerable.
Dealer North.

North	South
1♡	2♣
4♣	4♠
5NT	6♣

Not fancying the chances of establishing a trick in one of his long suits, West attacked with the nine of hearts. Dummy's ace won the trick as East followed with the two. The two of clubs was played from the table, and when East covered with the three South played for safety by finessing the four. He thus lost only one trump trick and made his slam.

East had cherished the hope that his queen of hearts might eventually score a trick, but he might have done better by trying for two trump tricks. What do you think would have happened if East had calmly dropped the queen of hearts under the ace at trick one?

Almost certainly South would have abandoned the safety-play in trumps for fear of losing to a singleton and suffering a ruff on the return. Instead South would have played a club to his ace. That would have given East two trump tricks and a story with which to bore his friends for weeks to come.

An aggressive early shift can sometimes have a similar effect.

```
                    ♠ A 7
                    ♡ 10 8 3
                    ◇ K 9 6 4
                    ♣ A Q 10 3
♠ Q 10 6 2                          ♠ J 8 5 4 3
♡ 6                                 ♡ K Q 4
◇ J 10 8 3                          ◇ A Q 5
♣ 9 8 5 4                           ♣ J 2
                    ♠ K 9
                    ♡ A J 9 7 5 2
                    ◇ 7 2
                    ♣ K 7 6
```

Both vulnerable.
Dealer South.

South	North
1 ♡	2 ♣
2 ♡	4 ♡

West finds the good lead of the jack of diamonds and declarer puts up dummy's king. East wins with the ace and cashes the queen of diamonds on which West plays the three. If a third diamond is played, declarer will ruff, enter dummy with the ace of spades and run the ten of hearts, making his contract for the loss of two diamonds and one heart.

It should be clear to East after the second trick that the only hope for the defense is to frighten declarer with the threat of a ruff. The way to do that is to shift to clubs at trick three. Either the jack or the two will do, provided that it is played promptly and with conviction.

What would you do in declarer's position after a club shift? It would look silly if you took a losing trump finesse and suffered a club ruff on the return. The natural thing for declarer to do is to abandon the trump finesse and play ace and another heart, relying on a 2-2 break or a singleton honor in one hand or the other.

A prompt shift was effective on this hand from the match between Norway and France in the European Championships of 1981.

```
              ♠ Q 9 4 3
              ♡ 9 5 4
              ◊ K 2
              ♣ Q J 10 4
♠ A J 2                        ♠ 10 8 7 6 5
♡ K 8                          ♡ J 7
◊ J 10 9 8 6 3                 ◊ A 5 4
♣ 9 7                          ♣ K 6 3
              ♠ K
              ♡ A Q 10 6 3 2
              ◊ Q 7
              ♣ A 8 5 2
```

East-West vulnerable.
Dealer East.

In both rooms South played in four hearts and received the lead of the jack of diamonds. The two was
played from the table, and in the Open Room Michel
Perron was allowed to win the first trick with the
queen. Lacking immediate entries to dummy, Perron
cashed the ace of hearts and then played the king of
spades. West took his ace, played a diamond to his
partner's ace, and won the trump return with the king.
That was the end of the road for the defense, however.
Dummy could not be kept off lead, and with the club
finesse right ten tricks rolled in.

In the Closed Room, where Phillipe Soulet occupied
the East seat, events took a different turn. Soulet
flashed up with the diamond ace at trick one and
whipped back the six of clubs. The threat of a club ruff
was worrying for declarer. If the six of clubs were a singleton, the contract could be made only if East had a
doubleton king of hearts. Convinced by the authority
of Soulet's play, South rose with the ace of clubs,
crossed to the king of diamonds and returned a heart
to his queen. A moment later he was entering minus
100 on his score card, for West won the king of hearts,
played a club to his partner's king and ruffed the club
return.

Time pressure is heavy in championship play, otherwise South might have come up with the right answer.
If East had really held the hand that South was playing
him for (K x in hearts and a singleton club), he would
not have allowed easy access to dummy for the heart
finesse by taking the ace of diamonds at trick one. The
only genuine chance was the club finesse, and South
should have played low from hand at trick two.

This in no way detracts from Soulet's imaginative
defense. It is always a good idea to make opponents
guess, for even at championship level they will sometimes guess wrong.

On certain hands instead of threatening declarer with a ruff you have to adopt the opposite policy of trying to convince him that the danger of a ruff is non-existent.

```
                  ♠ J 7 4
                  ♡ A 10 6 5
                  ◇ K Q J 6 3
                  ♣ 7
   ♠ 6 3                         ♠ A 10 8 5 2
   ♡ 9 2                         ♡ K 4 3
   ◇ 10 9                        ◇ 8 7 4 2
   ♣ A Q 9 8 6 4 2               ♣ 3
                  ♠ K Q 9
                  ♡ Q J 8 7
                  ◇ A 5
                  ♣ K J 10 5
```

Both vulnerable.
Dealer South.

South	North
1NT	2♣
2♡	4♡

Your lead of the ten of diamonds goes to the ace, and declarer runs the queen of hearts to partner's king. East returns the three of clubs on which South plays the jack.

Partner will need to have a spade trick to give you a chance, and the only possible source of a fourth defensive trick is a club ruff. You can be fairly sure that the three of clubs is a singleton, and your big advantage is that declarer cannot be aware of this.

However, if you win with the queen and continue with a low club, declarer will have to ruff in dummy and may well ruff high in order to avoid a blockage in trumps. Even if he ruffs low, partner may not be able to beat the six of hearts.

For the best chance of stealing an extra trick, win with the ace and return a low club. Declarer will then have no reason to ruff in dummy and may be lured to defeat.

There are times when a forcing defense is needed to defeat the contract. Try the next hand as a defensive problem.

```
        ♠ Q 5
        ♡ K J 3
        ◇ Q 10 5 4
        ♣ K 8 7 4
                        ♠ A 6 3 2
                        ♡ 10 8 2
                        ◇ A K 8 2
                        ♣ Q 3
```

North-South vulnerable.
Dealer East.

West	North	East	South
		1 ◇	Double
3 ◇	3NT	Pass	4 ♠
Pass	Pass	Pass	

West leads the three of diamonds and the ten is played from dummy. How do you defend?

You can count on a trick in diamonds and a trick in trumps, and partner is likely to have one of the missing aces. Where is the fourth defensive trick to come from? Your length in trumps suggests a forcing defense, but you can see that dummy's queen of diamonds will protect declarer from the force.

Are you sure about that? These things are all in the mind. It is obvious to you that declarer cannot be forced, but declarer does not know this because he is unaware of the location of all the diamond honors. This means that he *can* be forced after all. It may be a sort of phantom force, but declarer will have no way of distinguishing it from the real thing.

Win the first trick with the ace and return the two of diamonds. Declarer is sure to ruff, expecting your partner to have the king. When a trump is played to the queen, you plan to win at once and continue the deception by returning the eight of diamonds, 'forcing' declarer to ruff again.

The full hand:

```
                 ♠ Q 5
                 ♡ K J 3
                 ◇ Q 10 5 4
                 ♣ K 8 7 4
♠ 4                              ♠ A 6 3 2
♡ A 9 5                          ♡ 10 8 2
◇ J 9 6 3                        ◇ A K 8 2
♣ 10 9 6 5 2                     ♣ Q 3
                 ♠ K J 10 9 8 7
                 ♡ Q 7 6 4
                 ◇ 7
                 ♣ A J
```

You see what has happened? Even though declarer began with six trumps, he has now been reduced to the same number as you. He can draw your remaining trumps all right. But as soon as a heart is played West will take his ace and spoil South's day by playing the jack of diamonds to your king.

Declarer cannot possibly be blamed for falling for this ruse. For one thing, South knows that he can afford to accept the force when trumps are 3-2 and he has no reason to suspect a 4-1 break. If any declarer discards on the second round of diamonds, you would be well advised to hold your cards a bit closer to your chest.

Here is another case where the defenders can play

on their privileged knowledge of a bad trump break.

```
                    ♠ K 4
                    ♡ 6 5 2
                    ◇ Q 9 3
  ♠ J 10 8 6 5 3    ♣ A K Q 10 2    ♠ 7
  ♡ 4                               ♡ A 8 7 3
  ◇ 8 7 2                           ◇ A K J 6 5
  ♣ 9 5 4                           ♣ J 7 6
                    ♠ A Q 9 2
                    ♡ K Q J 10 9
                    ◇ 10 4
                    ♣ 8 3
```

Both vulnerable.
Dealer North.

West	North	East	South
	1♣	1◇	1♡
Pass	1NT	Pass	2♠
Pass	3♡	Pass	4♡
Pass	Pass	Pass	

West leads the eight of diamonds and declarer has to ruff the third round. The king of hearts is then played. How should East defend?

East may be tempted to hold off until the third round of trumps, after which he would be in a position to force declarer with a further diamond lead. A little sober reflection should tell him, however, that the third round of trumps will never come. When West shows out on the second trump, declarer will simply play one round of spades and then play on clubs, and East will be able to score no more than one trump trick.

The better idea is to win the first trump and play another diamond at once. Since West is out of trumps, it is safe for declarer to take the force in dummy. But

South docs not know this and will not risk discarding from hand in case West has the seven or eight of hearts. South is virtually certain to bank on a 3-2 trump break by ruffing in hand and trying to draw trumps, and East will score a long trump as the setting trick.

An illusion can sometimes be projected by ruffing with a higher trump than is necessary.

```
              ♠ 8 4 3
              ♡ 10 7 6 3
              ◇ A Q 8 5
              ♣ 8 7
♠ Q 5                        ♠ 9 7
♡ A 5                        ♡ K 9 8 4
◇ K 9 6 2                    ◇ J 10 4
♣ Q 10 6 4 3                 ♣ J 9 5 2
              ♠ A K J 10 6 2
              ♡ Q J 2
              ◇ 7 3
              ♣ A K
```

Both vulnerable.
Dealer South.

South	North
1♠	2♠
4♠	Pass

The defense started well when West hit upon the ace of hearts as his opening lead. East encouraged with the nine, won the next heart with the king and continued with the eight of hearts.

The chances of a fourth defensive trick did not appear to be too bright, so West tried the effect of ruffing the third heart with the queen of spades. He followed up with a prompt shift to the six of diamonds.

What would you have done? Understandably the declarer saw no reason to risk the diamond finesse. He went up with the ace and tried to cash the ten of hearts for a diamond discard. His faith in human nature received a rude jolt when West produced the five of spades to defeat the contract.

In the pairs game, where overtricks are beyond price, declarers are particularly vulnerable to this sort of trickery.

```
                    ♠ 7 6 2
                    ♡ 8 7
                    ◇ A Q J 10 4
                    ♣ A 8 6
  ♠ K Q J 9 4                        ♠ 10 8
  ♡ K 10 5                           ♡ 6 3
  ◇ 8                                ◇ 9 7 6 5 3 2
  ♣ K 7 5 4                          ♣ 10 9 2
                    ♠ A 5 3
                    ♡ A Q J 9 4 2
                    ◇ K
                    ♣ Q J 3
```

Match-point pairs.

Both vulnerable.
Dealer South.

South	West	North	East
1♡	1♠	2◇	Pass
3♡	Pass	4♡	Pass
Pass	Pass		

West led the king of spades to declarer's ace. Expecting the heart finesse to be wrong, South cashed the ace of hearts, overtook the king of diamonds with the ace and continued with the diamond queen, discarding a spade from hand. West calmly ruffed with the king of hearts, cashed the queen of spades and shifted to the five of clubs.

It is almost impossible for a declarer to smell out this kind of deception. West appeared to be marked with five clubs as well as five spades, but South saw no reason to risk the finesse since a gold-plated overtrick seemed assured by going up with the ace and discarding the losing clubs on the diamonds.

Someone should have had a camera at the ready when West ruffed the next diamond with the ten of hearts and took the setting trick with his king of clubs. South's expression was worth recording for posterity.

Greed for an overtrick has lured many a pairs player to his doom. On the next hand the defenders missed their way in the beginning but managed to recover when the declarer helped to bait a trap for himself.

```
                  ♠ 10 4 2
                  ♡ J 9 7 2
                  ◇ Q 7 3
                  ♣ K J 5
  ♠ A 6                          ♠ 9 8 5 3
  ♡ 4 3                          ♡ A 10 8 5
  ◇ K 8 5                        ◇ 4 2
  ♣ A 10 8 6 3 2                 ♣ Q 7 4
                  ♠ K Q J 7
                  ♡ K Q 6
                  ◇ A J 10 9 6
                  ♣ 9
```

Match-point pairs.

Both vulnerable.
Dealer South.

South	West	North	East
1 ◇	2 ♣	2 ◇	Pass
2 ♠	Pass	2NT	Pass
3 ◇	Pass	Pass	Pass

West led the four of hearts and the two was played from dummy. Obviously if East had ducked he could later have given his partner a ruff, but the position was not too easy to read and in practice East played the ace and another heart. South unblocked his queen and won the second heart with dummy's seven. He then led the queen of diamonds and played the nine from his hand.

In with the king of diamonds, West paused to review the situation. Since South clearly had five diamonds, his play of the nine had to be an unblocking move made in the hope of gaining entry to dummy on the third round of trumps. South must, in fact, be hoping to discard a singleton club on the fourth round of hearts. West decided to encourage this ambition by returning the eight of diamonds.

From declarer's point of view, West appeared to be marked with doubletons in both red suits. After winning the second trump, therefore, South judged it safe to unblock the king of hearts. Thus West got his heart ruff after all, and he promptly cashed the black aces to put the contract one down.

There is scope for deception when a defender has the chance to over-ruff dummy.

```
                    ♠ K 9 4
                    ♡ Q 8 7 2
                    ◊ 9 7
                    ♣ K J 5 2
♠ J 8 6                              ♠ 10 7 5 3
♡ 4                                  ♡ K J 5 3
◊ K Q 10 8 5 3                       ◊ A 2
♣ 8 7 4                              ♣ 10 9 6
                    ♠ A Q 2
                    ♡ A 10 9 6
                    ◊ J 6 4
                    ♣ A Q 3
```

East-West vulnerable.
Dealer South.

South	North
1NT	2♣
2♡	4♡

The opening lead was the king of diamonds. East overtook with the ace and returned the two of diamonds to his partner's ten. At trick three the queen of diamonds was ruffed in dummy with the seven of hearts and the ball was in East's court.

There appeared to be little chance of a trick for the defense in the black suits, and East decided that he would need to score two trumps. Accordingly, he over-ruffed the third diamond with the king of hearts and shifted to a club.

Declarer can hardly be blamed for assuming the jack of hearts to be with West. Winning the club in hand, he cashed the ace of hearts and continued with the six, intending to run it if West followed with a small heart. But West showed out and the contract had to go one down.

Note that if East had over-ruffed with the heart jack at trick three he would have left declarer with no alternative to the winning play of running the queen of hearts on the second round.

On certain hands the tricky game may be to refuse to over-ruff.

```
                    ♠ K 3
                    ♡ A J 6
                    ♦ A 10 9 6 5 2
                    ♣ 9 4
    ♠ J 8 4 2                        ♠ 10 9 6
    ♡ 10 3                           ♡ K 7 5
    ♦ K J 4                          ♦ 8 3
    ♣ A Q 7 2       ♠ A Q 7 5        ♣ J 10 6 5 3
                    ♡ Q 9 8 4 2
                    ♦ Q 7
                    ♣ K 8
```

Both vulnerable.
Dealer South.

South	North
1♡	2◊
2♡	4♡

A trump lead would have made declarer's task too difficult, but West chose to attack with the two of spades. South played three rounds of spades, discarding a club from the table, and then played the queen of diamonds. This was covered by the king and ace, and the ten of diamonds was returned to the jack.

After cashing the ace of clubs West played the jack of spades, which was ruffed in dummy with the jack of hearts. East discarded a club as though he had no problem, after which declarer was fated to take the wrong view in trumps. He cashed the ace of hearts and continued with the six, on which East played low. Believing the king to be on his left, South finessed the eight and lost to West's ten.

If East had over-ruffed with the king of hearts on the fourth round of spades, that would have been the last trick for the defense.

Here is a final hand to round off the theme of larceny in the trump suit.

```
                    ♠ A Q J 10 3
                    ♡ 4 2
                    ◊ 8 6 4
  ♠ K 9 5 2         ♣ J 10 6        ♠ 8 7 4
  ♡ K J                             ♡ 8 5
  ◊ A K Q 7                         ◊ 10 9 5 3
  ♣ 9 5 4           ♠ 6             ♣ K 8 7 2
                    ♡ A Q 10 9 7 6 3
                    ◊ J 2
                    ♣ A Q 3
```

Both vulnerable.
Dealer South.

South	West	North	East
1♡	Double	1♠	Pass
3♡	Pass	4♡	Pass
Pass	Pass		

West attacked in diamonds and declarer ruffed the third round. With only one entry in dummy, South saw that he could not finesse in both hearts and clubs. Rightly he took the view that the club finesse offered the best chance, and he decided to tackle the trumps by playing out the ace and another, hoping for a 2-2 break or a singleton honor.

On the lie of the cards this line of play was destined to succeed, but West found a way of giving destiny a black eye when he dropped the king of hearts under the ace. There was little risk in this play for South was unlikely to have more than seven hearts, and West expected the sacrificed trick to come back with interest.

That is how it worked out. Convinced that he could now make his contract without risking the club finesse, South crossed to the ace of spades and returned the heart for a finesse of the ten. But West produced the jack of hearts and exited with a diamond, and South was unable to avoid a club loser.

Chapter 9

TURNING THE SCREW

In the four chapters in which we have espoused the declarer's cause we have discovered so many ways of baffling the defenders that by now they should be bewitched, bothered and bewildered and ready to cry for mercy. Yet to judge from the evidence of the last chapter they are still fighting back with fiendish cunning. Clearly it is time to step up the pace, to put the opponents under such relentless pressure that they have little chance of working out the right defense.

A good way of concealing a weakness elsewhere in your hand is by masking your strength in the suit first attacked. The choice of card played from dummy can often influence the result.

A Q 5

J 2

When West leads a small card in this suit, it seems natural to play low from dummy. That way you will make three tricks in the suit if West has led away from the king. But suppose you need only two tricks in the suit. Now it is more sensible to play the queen from dummy at trick one, making it attractive for East to return the suit if he happens to have the king.

The late Ewart Kempson, former editor of Bridge Magazine and a great player of the cards, claimed to have invented this ruse and called it the Kempson Coup. I am quite willing to go along with that, and the Kempson Coup is certainly worth a trick or two when the conditions are right.

Here it is in the context of a complete deal.

```
                    ♠ A K 10 7 4
                    ♡ A Q 3
                    ◊ J 6
                    ♣ K Q 4
  ♠ 9 3                              ♠ Q J 6 2
  ♡ 10 8 7 5 2                       ♡ K 9 6
  ◊ K 7 2                            ◊ A Q 10 3
  ♣ 7 6 3                            ♣ 9 2
                    ♠ 8 5
                    ♡ J 4
                    ◊ 9 8 5 4
                    ♣ A J 10 8 5
```

North-South vulnerable.
Dealer North.

West	North	East	South
	1♠	Pass	1NT
Pass	3NT	Pass	Pass
Pass			

The opening lead is the five of hearts. If West has led away from the king you can make three heart tricks by running the lead to your jack. But you have no need of three heart tricks; two will suffice for your contract. So don't be greedy. Play the queen of hearts from dummy just in case the king is lurking in the East hand. On winning with the king, East will entertain hopes of setting up at least one more heart trick, and he may well continue with the nine of hearts.

If you play low from dummy at trick one, informing East that you have two tricks in hearts, he is much more likely to find the shift to the queen of diamonds at trick two, striking oil in his partner's hand. West will encourage with the seven, and the defenders will take the first five tricks to put your contract one down.

Sometimes it takes the play of an unexpected card to give a defender the green light.

```
                    ♠ 8 7 4
                    ♡ A 4
                    ◊ A Q J 9 4
                    ♣ J 7 5
  ♠ K Q 10 9 5                      ♠ 6 2
  ♡ 10 7                            ♡ J 9 6 2
  ◊ 7 6 5                           ◊ K 8 3
  ♣ Q 8 3                           ♣ K 10 9 4
                    ♠ A J 3
                    ♡ K Q 8 5 3
                    ◊ 10 2
                    ♣ A 6 2
```

Both vulnerable.
Dealer South.

South	West	North	East
1 ♡	Pass	2 ◊	Pass
2NT	Pass	3NT	Pass
Pass	Pass		

West leads the king of spades against your contract of three notrumps. How do you plan the play?

Obviously you cannot afford to win the first trick, since you have to take the diamond finesse into the East hand and a spade return from East would be fraught with danger. An alternative is to play the three of spades at trick one, but that is not completely satisfactory either. West will no doubt have heard of the Bath Coup and will not continue the suit but look for another angle of attack. And a club shift from West would be far from welcome.

That leaves only one other card for you to consider, and a very good card it is. The play of the jack of spades at trick one makes it 'safe' for West to continue the suit and he is likely to do so, thinking that hc has you on the run. You can win the second spade and finesse in diamonds with complete safety. On a 4-3 spade break you have no objection to losing three spades and a diamond, and if the spades are 5-2 East will not have one to return.

Of course, you are not likely to get away with this against defenders who give count signals on the lead of the king. Knowing that his partner would not drop the six from 6 3 2, West will realise that you have concealed a low card and may well find the deadly club shift. For all that, the play is still worth trying, for defenders sometimes fail to notice their partners' signals.

Another way of diverting attention from your real weakness is by pretending to have a quick loser in the suit first attacked.

```
                    ♠ K 8 7 5 3
                    ♡ K 10 4
                    ◊ Q 6 5
                    ♣ A 10
♠ --                                  ♠ 10 4
♡ A J 8 6 2                           ♡ Q 9 5 3
◊ J 10 9 7 2                          ◊ K 8 4 3
♣ 7 5 4                              ♣ K 6 2
                    ♠ A Q J 9 6 2
                    ♡ 7
                    ◊ A
                    ♣ Q J 9 8 3
```

Both vulnerable.
Dealer South.

South	West	North	East
1 ♠	Pass	3 ♠	Pass
6 ♠	Pass	Pass	Pass

The bidding may be less than scientific but at least it gives little away. West leads the jack of diamonds against your slam. How should you play?

It looks as though the slam depends on the success of the club finesse. However, players rarely lead from interior sequences against a slam and you can be confident that East will have the king of diamonds. That suggests a way of giving yourself an extra chance when the club finesse is wrong. Cover the jack of diamonds with dummy's queen, capture East's king with your ace, and immediately lead the queen of clubs for a finesse (not a low club, which would provide a clue to your length in the suit).

Now when East wins with the king he may try to cash a diamond trick, in which case all dummy's hearts will eventually be discarded on your clubs.

Note the vital importance of taking the club finesse at trick two, before drawing trumps. If you cash even one round of trumps West will seize the opportunity to discard the jack of hearts, after which his partner will not go wrong. Even if West pulls the wrong card, dropping the three of hearts on the first trump, the knowledge that you have six spades is in itself enough to enable East to work out that a heart return cannot possibly hurt the defense.

It is a matter of basic technique on such hands to make your deceptive play at the earliest possible moment. Unfortunately, the technique has an inherent flaw, since a perceptive defender in the East seat will ask himself why you have not made the obvious play of drawing trumps. If he reaches the conclusion that you are terrified of a signal from someone, he may do the right thing after all.

We have already seen Tim Seres of Australia at work in a defensive role. Here he is as declarer bringing home an impossible slam.

```
                    ♠ K 7 4
                    ♡ A 9 8 7
                    ◇ A 9 7 4 3
                    ♣ Q
♠ Q J 10 3                              ♠ 9 8 6 5
♡ 4                                     ♡ 5 3
◇ J 10 6                                ◇ Q 8
♣ 10 8 6 5 2                            ♣ A 9 7 4 3
                    ♠ A 2
                    ♡ K Q J 10 6 2
                    ◇ K 5 2
                    ♣ K J
```

Neither vulnerable.
Dealer North.

West	North	East	South
	1 ◇	Pass	1 ♡
Pass	2 ♡	Pass	4NT
Pass	5 ♡	Pass	6 ♡
Pass	Pass	Pass	

West led the queen of spades and it was immediately clear that there was no genuine play for the slam since there were losers in both minor suits. West might not realise this, however, and Seres decided that his only chance was to trade on West's ignorance. He played low from dummy at trick one and low again from his own hand.

Thinking he had struck it rich, West naturally continued with a second spade and the rest was easy. After drawing trumps, Seres cashed the top diamonds, discarded his diamond loser on the king of spades, and ruffed a diamond in hand. When he had entered dummy with a trump, he was able to discard both of his clubs on the established diamonds.

Many players since have brought off similar swindles and the ruse is now well known, but Seres played the above hand thirty years ago when such a coup was almost unheard of.

When declarer refuses to win a trick that he could have won, it can be hard for the defenders to figure out what is going on.

```
                    ♠ A 9 6 5
                    ♡ 4
                    ◇ K Q 9 6 3 2
                    ♣ 7 5
♠ K Q J 8                                ♠ 10 4 3 2
♡ 8 6 5                                  ♡ A 9
◇ J 4                                    ◇ 10 8 7 5
♣ Q 9 6 2                                ♣ K 10 3
                    ♠ 7
                    ♡ K Q J 10 7 3 2
                    ◇ A
                    ♣ A J 8 4
```

Both vulnerable.
Dealer South.

South	West	North	East
1♡	Pass	2◇	Pass
4♡	Pass	Pass	Pass

West leads the king of spades, inconveniently attacking dummy's entry to the long diamonds. You are not going to be allowed to ruff a club with dummy's lone heart, and the only genuine chance of making the contract is to find one of the defenders with K Q x in clubs.

That is a slender chance and the better shot is to trade on West's ignorance of your blocked diamond position by playing low from dummy at trick one. This is not without its dangers, for if West shifts at trick two you may never make a spade trick and may finish two down. However, it is long odds that West will continue the spade attack, intent on knocking out the entry before you can establish any tricks in diamonds.

The spade continuation makes things easy for you. The blocking ace of diamonds goes away on the spade ace, and two of your losing clubs are discarded on the king and queen of diamonds. Now it is time to play trumps, and you lose no more than one trump trick, one spade and one club.

A good way of masking a weakness elsewhere in your hand is to win the first trick twice over.

```
                    ♠ A 7
                    ♡ 9 7 6
                    ◇ Q 10 4 3
                    ♣ A 10 6 3
♠ J 10 9 6 5                    ♠ 8 4 3
♡ A 10 5 2                      ♡ K Q 4
◇ K 8                          ◇ 7 5 2
♣ 8 5                          ♣ 9 7 4 2
                    ♠ K Q 2
                    ♡ J 8 3
                    ◇ A J 9 6
                    ♣ K Q J
```

Both vulnerable.
Dealer South.

South	West	North	East
1NT	Pass	3NT	Pass
Pass	Pass		

West leads the jack of spades, and you see that eleven tricks will be there for the taking if the diamond finesse is right. The hearts are wide open, however, and West may find the shift if he has the king of diamonds.

Since you have no need of eleven tricks, or even ten, you should try to convince West that it is spades rather than hearts that represents the main chance for the defense. Win the first trick with the ace of spades and drop the spade queen from your hand.

Since the card concealed is the two, it will appear to West that his partner has started an echo with four cards in the suit. When the diamond finesse loses, West is virtually certain to continue spades, intent on establishing the suit while he still has the ace of hearts as an entry. From West's point of view this defense must defeat the contract unless you have four tricks in clubs, and he will think it more likely that his partner has one honor in clubs than two in hearts.

This type of play has many variations. Try the next hand as a single-dummy problem.

♠ K 8 3
♥ Q 10
♦ J 7 4   North-South vulnerable.
♣ A 10 9 5 2   Dealer South.

	South	North
♠ A Q 5	1NT	3NT
♥ A J 2		
♦ 9 5 3		
♣ K J 6 4		

West leads the four of hearts and East plays the five under dummy's queen. Quick! How do you play?

You should, of course, have thought the whole thing through before playing the queen of hearts from the table. With two tricks in hearts and three in spades, you need four tricks from the club suit. The clubs will yield four tricks all right, but the danger is that the defenders will be able to score at least four tricks in diamonds if you let them in.

It looks at though the contract will be made only if you can bring in the clubs without loss, but this is not necessarily the case. It depends on how attractive you make it for the defenders to continue hearts. The tricky play is to drop the jack of hearts under dummy's queen an take a first-round club finesse towards West.

The complete deal may be:

```
                    ♠ K 8 3
                    ♡ Q 10
                    ◊ J 7 4
                    ♣ A 10 9 5 2
♠ J 6                               ♠ 10 9 7 4 2
♡ K 9 8 4 3                         ♡ 7 6 5
◊ A 10 2                            ◊ K Q 8 6
♣ Q 8 3                             ♣ 7
                    ♠ A Q 5
                    ♡ A J 2
                    ◊ 9 5 3
                    ♣ K J 6 4
```

The club finesse loses, but West is unlikely to find the diamond shift. For all he knows this might present you with your ninth trick. It will appear to West that his partner has started an echo to show four hearts, and it will be unnatural for him to do anything other than continue with the king of hearts at trick three.

Note the importance of finessing on the first round of clubs. If you cash the club ace before taking the finesse, you give East the opportunity to discard a heart. Now West, on seeing his partner play hearts upwards, will realise that you are up to some knavery and will probably find the diamond shift.

Well done if you spotted the best play, but that is only half the problem. To earn full marks you should have had a plan of campaign ready in case East covered the queen of hearts with the king at trick one.

The appearance of the king gives you a third trick in hearts, but you still need an extra trick in clubs for your contract. If you win the first trick with the ace of hearts, both opponents are likely to realise that you have a second stopper in the suit. Otherwise you would surely have held up the ace. If you have to lose a club trick, either East or West may find the deadly diamond shift.

This time your best shot is to drop the two of hearts under the king. East will no doubt continue the suit, in which case you will win with the jack and play a low club for a finesse of dummy's nine.

The full hand could be:

```
                    ♠  K 8 3
                    ♡  Q 10
                    ◇  J 7 4
                    ♣  A 10 9 5 2
  ♠  J 7 6 2                        ♠  10 9 4
  ♡  9 7 6 4 3                      ♡  K 8 5
  ◇  A 10 2                         ◇  K Q 8 6
  ♣  8                              ♣  Q 7 3
                    ♠  A Q 5
                    ♡  A J 2
                    ◇  9 5 3
                    ♣  K J 6 4
```

After winning the queen of clubs East is likely to continue with a third heart under the impression that you began with J 9 2 and his partner with A 7 6 4 3.

Again note that the value of the first-round finesse in clubs, denying West the chance to signal with the ten of diamonds. You willingly trade a small portion of your technical chances for a psychological advantage.

You would probably get away with this swindle against most defenders, but an expert West would play the nine of hearts on the second round, exposing your deception. If that happened you would have to forget about the first-round club finesse and concentrate on the best chance of bringing in the club suit without loss. Since East is marked with three hearts to West's five, the odds favour a second-round finesse through East.

When there is a possibility of establishing an extra trick by means of a loser-on-loser play, the defenders may be persuaded to attack the wrong suit if you make it a winner-on-loser play instead. This ruse may be well known but it is still good for plenty of tricks.

```
                    ♠ K J 4
                    ♡ Q 8 3
                    ◇ Q J 5 4
                    ♣ Q 9 2
   ♠ 10 5                          ♠ 8 3
   ♡ K 10 6                        ♡ A J 7 4
   ◇ A K 10 6 2                    ◇ 9 7 3
   ♣ 8 7 4                         ♣ J 10 6 5
                    ♠ A Q 9 7 6 2
                    ♡ 9 5 2
                    ◇ 8
                    ♣ A K 3
```

North-South vulnerable.
Dealer West.

West	North	East	South
Pass	Pass	Pass	1 ♠
Pass	2NT	Pass	4 ♠
Pass	Pass	Pass	

West starts with the king of diamonds and shifts to the eight of clubs, which is covered by the nine, ten and ace. How should you continue?

West is marked with the top diamonds but he passed originally, so it is no good hoping for him to have the ace and king of hearts as well. The only chance is to establish a tenth trick in diamonds. Cross to the king of spades and play the queen of diamonds, discarding not a heart but the three of clubs from your hand.

This exposes you to the risk of going two down, but it is a risk worth taking. In practice West may well continue clubs, hoping to defeat the contract with one trick in clubs and one in hearts. If he does, you are in a position to draw trumps and discard two of your heart losers on the minor suit winners in dummy.

The defenders are not without ways of protecting themselves in these situations. When the queen of diamonds is played from dummy, East should play the nine as a suit-preference signal asking for a heart shift. But players often do not think of such things until it is too late.

Fourth Hand High

A stratagem that is practically guaranteed to succeed is to win a trick with a higher card than is strictly necessary. Here is a well-known situation.

```
                    ♠ 8 6 5
                    ♡ 7 5
                    ◊ Q J 8 4
                    ♣ Q 9 6 2
      ♠ K 9 4                        ♠ A 10 7 3 2
      ♡ K 10 8 6 2                   ♡ J 9 3
      ◊ 9 5                          ◊ 10 6 2
      ♣ K 8 3                        ♣ 7 4
                    ♠ Q J
                    ♡ A Q 4
                    ◊ A K 7 3
                    ♣ A J 10 5
```

Both vulnerable.
Dealer South.

South	West	North	East
2NT	Pass	3NT	Pass
Pass	Pass		

West leads the six of hearts to his partner's jack, and you see that it is the same old story--one suit wide open. Mind you, no other game would have much of a chance, and you will make plenty of tricks if the club finesse is right.

When the club finesse is wrong, however, West may well shift to spades, putting the contract one or two down. To deflect him from this course, you should win the first trick with the ace of hearts, concealing the queen.

If West still finds the spade shift after winning the king of clubs, you will soon be writing minus 600 on your card, a figure that will take some explaining to your team-mates. But in real life it will never happen. Convinced that the heart suit is his to run, West will play another small heart to his partner's 'marked' queen, thereby giving you back your ninth trick.

Plays of this type are worth considering whenever you expect West to win the first trick for the defense.

5

A Q 9 4 2   10 8 3

K J 7 6

When West leads the four and East plays the ten, try the effect of winning with the king instead of the jack. It will make no difference to the result if East gains the lead, but if West comes in he is likely to give you a second trick in the suit, either by leading a low card towards his partner's supposed jack or by playing the suit from the top, expecting his partner to unblock.

Here is another case.

7 6
Q 9 8 4 3   10 5 2
                  A K J

Again West leads the four and East plays the ten. Win with the king if you fear a shift to another suit. The trick that you appear to be giving up will come back when West is next on lead.

A curious example of this type of play comes from a Philip Morris Cup heat in Zurich some years ago. The deal features the late Leon Yallouze of France, who was a popular and respected competitor on the European bridge scene.

```
                    ♠ 9 5 3 2
                    ♡ K 8
                    ◇ K 6 3 2
                    ♣ 10 5 3
  ♠ A 8 6                          ♠ K Q 7 4
  ♡ Q 6 4 3                        ♡ 7 2
  ◇ Q 8 5                          ◇ 9 7 4
  ♣ A 8 4                          ♣ K Q 9 6
                    ♠ J 10
                    ♡ A J 10 9 5
                    ◇ A J 10
                    ♣ J 7 2
```

Match-point pairs.
Neither vulnerable.
Dealer South.

South	West	North	East
1♡	Pass	1♠	Pass
1NT	Pass	Pass	Pass

This contract was popular but seldom successful, since the defenders can take the first eight tricks if they start with one of the black suits.

When Yallouze was the declarer West led the five of diamonds, which drew the two, the nine and the ace! Declarer crossed to the king of hearts and finessed the jack on the way back, losing to the queen of hearts. Duly taken in, West continued with the eight of diamonds which ran to the ten, giving Yallouze eight tricks for a big score.

Clearly if declarer had won the first trick with the ten or jack of diamonds it would have been easy for West to find a shift when in with the queen of hearts. Perhaps he should have shifted anyway, for there could hardly be a bonanza for the defense in diamonds even if East had the jack and ten.

But the main blame for the misdefense belonged to East. What was he trying to promote with his nine of diamonds? If East plays the four of diamonds on the first trick declarer has no opportunity for deception.

Chapter 10

PUTTING THE BOOT IN

So far we have been treating declarer fairly gently. We've been fooling him, to be sure, but the fooling has been done in a sporting manner without any hard feelings. All this must change now that we know from the last chapter about the dirty tricks declarer has in store for us. Declarer is not the only one with a box of tricks at his disposal. From now on our aim must be to step up the pressure by putting declarer to an awkward guess whenever we possibly can.

Opportunities for creating a losing option arise when declarer forces us to open up a new suit in the later stages of the play. Usually it is an end-play situation where you cannot afford to return any other suit, and if declarer knew the position of the cards he would never get it wrong.

<table>
<tr><td></td><td>A 10 3</td><td></td></tr>
<tr><td>Q 8 5</td><td></td><td>J 7 6 2</td></tr>
<tr><td></td><td>K 9 4</td><td></td></tr>
</table>

If you have to tackle this suit from the West hand, do not take the soft option of playing a low card. That would leave declarer with no choice but the winning line of playing for split honors. Lead the queen to give declarer a guess. He may still get it right by playing for split honors, but he may also go wrong by playing you for Q J x.

The position is no different if you have to open up the suit from the East hand. The only way to give declarer a guess is to lead the jack.

```
              J 9 3
K 10 5                      Q 7 6 2
              A 8 4
```

In this common position if you have to broach the suit from the East hand the best card to play is the queen. Declarer may well play low, placing you with K Q 10.

Tackling the suit from the West hand, you should normally lead the king. Declarer may do the right thing by winning with the ace and finessing the nine next time, but he may go astray by placing you with K Q x. Against a sophisticated declarer you might try a lead of the five from the West hand. Expecting you to lead the king from K 10 5, declarer may put you with K Q 5 and go up with the jack from dummy.

Declarer's inability to see through the backs of the cards means that he can sometimes be swindled out of a trick that is rightfully his.

```
              K 8 3
A Q 9 4                     J 6 2
              10 7 5
```

A bold lead of the queen from the West hand gives the declarer a tricky problem in situations like this. If he gets it right by going up with the king you have lost nothing. And if he plays low from dummy on the first round, you can play on his nerves by continuing with the four. This time he loses his trick in the suit if he gets it wrong.

Should South cover the queen when it is led? If he does, he may discover that the position is as follows:

```
                K 8 3
Q J 9 4                              A 6 2
                10 7 5
```

You lead the queen in this position as well, and now it is fatal for declarer to cover with the king.

Should South play low from dummy on the first round and rely on making the right guess when you continue with the four? This does not guarantee success either, for the true position may be as shown below.

```
                K 8 3
Q 9 6 4                              A J 2
                10 7 5
```

Again you lead the queen from the West hand. This time the only way for declarer to salvage his trick is to play the king on the first round and go up with the ten when East returns the two.

The defenders have the advantage in such situations, for it is not easy for declarer to do the right thing. If you force him to guess, he is sure to guess wrong some of the time.

In the next position declarer can always make two tricks if he knows where the cards lie, but for all that he may be held to one trick.

```
                K 8 3
10 7 4 2                             A J 5
                Q 9 6
```

If East has to tackle the suit, the right card to play is the jack. Declarer may go wrong by winning in dummy with the king and finessing the nine on the way back.

From the West hand a lead of the ten may work well, since declarer may suspect this of being a tricky card from J 10 x.

Let us view a similar matrix in the setting of a complete hand.

```
                    ♠ Q 8 7 4 2
                    ♡ Q 9 2
                    ◇ A K 10
                    ♣ J 7
♠ K J                               ♠ 5
♡ A 10 6                            ♡ J 7 3
◇ 9 7 6 2                           ◇ Q J 8 4
♣ K 10 5 3                          ♣ Q 8 6 4 2
                    ♠ A 10 9 6 3
                    ♡ K 8 5 4
                    ◇ 5 3
                    ♣ A 9
```

Both vulnerable.
Dealer South.

South	West	North	East
1 ♠	Pass	3 ♠	Pass
4 ♠	Pass	Pass	Pass

You lead the seven of diamonds to dummy's king. South plays a spade to his ace, returns to the ace of diamonds, ruffs the ten of diamonds in hand, cashes the ace of clubs, and exits with his second club which you wisely win with the king.

After cashing the king of spades you know South's distribution to be 5-4-2-2. You cannot afford to concede a ruff and discard, and it is clear that you need two tricks from the heart suit. South is marked with the king of hearts, and you have to hope that partner has the jack. It is not good enough to lead the six of hearts at this point. South will capture the jack with his king and will have no way of going wrong on the next round.

The only way to give declarer a guess is to lead the ten of hearts. Now South may go astray by winning in hand and finessing dummy's nine when you play low on the second round.

Fourth Hand High

If it can sometimes be profitable for declarer to win a trick with a higher card than is strictly necessary, the same should hold for the defenders. So it does. The move is particularly effective when it deflects declarer from a winning finesse and persuades him to repeat a losing one. Here is an example.

```
                 ♠ J 7 5 3
                 ♡ A K J 3 2
                 ◊ J 9 3
                 ♣ 9
 ♠ 10 4 2                        ♠ Q 9 8
 ♡ Q 8 5                         ♡ 10 6 4
 ◊ A Q                           ◊ 7 5 4
 ♣ Q 10 8 4 2                    ♣ J 7 5 3
                 ♠ A K 6
                 ♡ 9 7
                 ◊ K 10 8 6 2
                 ♣ A K 6
```

Both vulnerable.
Dealer South.

South	North
1NT	2♣
2◊	3♡
3NT	Pass

West leads the four of clubs to the jack and king. Crossing to dummy with the king of hearts, South runs the nine of diamonds. The natural defense is to win with the queen and clear the clubs, but if West does that the declarer is bound to make his contract. On winning the ace of clubs he will take his only remaining chance by finessing in hearts, and the favorable lie of the cards will give him nine tricks.

To create a losing option West should win the first diamond with the ace. Leaving the queen exposed is less dangerous than it seems, for South is virtually certain to go wrong. Believing the diamond finesse to be working, he will reject the heart finesse as an unnecessary risk. After winning the ace of clubs he will play a heart to the ace and run the jack of diamonds, and that will be two down.

A good example of this type of swindle came up in the 1980 Spingold Teams.

```
                    ♠ K J 10 9 7 5
                    ♡ 8 4
                    ◇ J 10 8
                    ♣ K 4
♠ 3 2                                   ♠ A Q 6
♡ 10 6 2                                ♡ J 9 7 5
◇ 9 3 2                                 ◇ A Q 5
♣ Q J 9 8 7                             ♣ 10 3 2
                    ♠ 8 4
                    ♡ A K Q 3
                    ◇ K 7 6 4
                    ♣ A 6 5
```

Both vulnerable.
Dealer South.

South opened one notrump and eventually played in four spades after a transfer response from North. The opening lead of the queen of clubs was won by the ace.

A study of all four hands shows that there are just three tricks for the defense--two spades and a diamond. Since East has both ace and queen of diamonds there is no chance of declarer taking a wrong view in the suit, and dummy's third diamond can always be discarded on the third round of hearts. There appears to be no way for the defenders to score a fourth trick.

World Champion Mike Passell occupied the East seat, however, and he found a way. When declarer played a spade for a finesse at trick two, Passell won with the ace. He cashed the ace of diamonds (on which his partner John Mohan played the nine) and continued with the five of diamonds, which South naturally won with the king.

Declarer would still have been all right if he had played three rounds of hearts and discarded the losing diamond from dummy. He saw no reason to risk an adverse ruff before drawing trumps, however, and played another trump to take the 'proven' finesse. You can imagine his dismay when Passell produced the queen of spades and took the setting trick with the queen of diamonds.

It is always hard for declarers to believe that a defender has won with a high card when a lower one would have done. Here is another case.

	♠ K Q 9	
	♡ A 10 8 3	
	◊ K 7 5	
	♣ A K 5	
♠ 10 7 2		♠ J 6 5 3
♡ K J 7 4		♡ 6 2
◊ Q 10 8 3		◊ A 9 2
♣ 8 4		♣ Q J 9 3
	♠ A 8 4	
	♡ Q 9 5	
	◊ J 6 4	
	♣ 10 7 6 2	

Both vulnerable.
Dealer North.

North	South
1 ♡	1NT
3NT	Pass

West led the three of diamonds to his partner's ace. The nine of diamonds was returned and declarer held up dummy's king until the third round. Needing three tricks from the heart suit, South played the three of hearts from the table and put in the nine from hand.

Seeing a slim chance of scoring a second heart trick, West made a quick decision to conceal his jack. He won with the king, cashed the queen of diamonds and exited with a club.

What would you have done in declarer's place? Convinced that the jack of hearts was with East, South led and ran the eight of hearts from dummy, and that was five tricks for the defense.

If West had played naturally by winning the first heart with the jack, declarer would have been left with no alternative to the winning play of running the queen of hearts on the next round.

When the next hand turned up in a pairs tournament the contract of six spades was normally made in great comfort. But at one table the declarer had the misfortune to run into an imaginative defense.

```
                  ♠ K Q 10 4
                  ♡ 5
                  ◇ K J 10 9 3
                  ♣ K 8 6
  ♠ 8 5 2                          ♠ 6 3
  ♡ Q J 10 9 2                     ♡ K 3
  ◇ 6 4                            ◇ A Q 7 5 2
  ♣ 10 7 3                         ♣ 9 5 4 2
                  ♠ A J 9 7
                  ♡ A 8 7 6 4
                  ◇ 8
                  ♣ A Q J
```

Match-point pairs.
Both vulnerable.
Dealer South.

South	North
1 ♡	2 ◇
2 ♠	3 ♣
4 ♣	4NT
5 ♠	6 ♠

The lead of the queen of hearts went to the ace, and the declarer immediately ran the eight of diamonds. Since it was clear from the bidding that this was a singleton, East casually won with the ace and returned the king of hearts for dummy to ruff.

Believing the queen of diamonds to be with West, South thought he could see twelve tricks on a cross-ruff without risking more than two rounds of clubs. After a club to the ace and a club back to the king, he discarded the queen of clubs on the king of diamonds and then ruffed a diamond with the seven of spades. His jaw dropped several inches when West over-ruffed to defeat the slam.

At the other tables where East won the first diamond with the queen the declarers could not go wrong. Where trumps had been led initially, they drew trumps and relied on finding the diamond ace with East. Some of those who had escaped trump leads preferred to cash three clubs and cross-ruff the rest. Both methods produced twelve tricks.

An unusual case of fourth-hand high made an appearance in the match between Brazil and Turkey at the 1980 Teams Olympiad.

```
              ♠ A K 2
              ♡ K 6 3 2
              ◇ Q 10 6 5 3
              ♣ K
♠ 9 4                          ♠ 7 6 5 3
♡ 10 9 7                       ♡ J 8 5 4
◇ A 8                          ◇ K J
♣ A Q J 8 4 2                  ♣ 10 7 6
              ♠ Q J 10 8
              ♡ A Q
              ◇ 9 7 4 2
              ♣ 9 5 3
```

North-South vulnerable.
Dealer West.

West	North	East	South
Assumpcao		Chagas	
2♣	Double	Pass	3♠
Pass	4♠	Pass	Pass
Pass			

West led the ten of hearts to South's ace, and the declarer realised that he had to tackle the diamonds while dummy still had trumps to take care of a club force. When a low diamond was led, West went up with the ace, and Gabriel Chagas in the East seat smoothly dropped the king!

Completely deceived, the declarer won the heart return, drew trumps and played a diamond to the ten, expecting to make an overtrick. But Chagas produced the jack and returned a club to give his partner the rest of the tricks.

All credit to Chagas for his imaginative defense, but the declarer was a little too innocent. It was unlikely that a player of the stature of Pedro Paul Assumpcao would go up with the ace of diamonds from A J 8. And if he *had* done that, why did he not continue with a diamond for his partner to ruff, win the club return with the ace, and give East another diamond ruff?

There is quite an art in deflecting a declarer from the winning course. On the next hand the declarer was well on the way to making his contract when a funny thing happened.

```
                    ♠ J 9
                    ♡ A K J 10
                    ◇ K 6 3
                    ♣ K 4 3 2
  ♠ Q 10 8 7 4                        ♠ K 6 5 2
  ♡ Q 7 2                             ♡ 6 5 3
  ◇ Q 10 5                            ◇ 8 4 2
  ♣ J 7                               ♣ Q 10 6
                    ♠ A 3
                    ♡ 9 8 4
                    ◇ A J 9 7
                    ♣ A 9 8 5
```

Neither vulnerable.
Dealer South.

South	North
1 ◇	1 ♡
1NT	3NT

The opening lead of the seven of spades was covered by the jack and king and won by South with the ace. Declarer counted seven top tricks and decided that the heart finesse offered the best chance of scoring the extra tricks he needed for the contract. However, being a careful player who liked to give himself all the chances, he first played a heart to the ace and then played off the king and ace of diamonds to see what that would produce.

It produced something very interesting. On the second round of diamonds West dropped the queen! South was delighted at this development, for he could now see his way to making nine tricks without risk. Rejecting the heart finesse, he entered dummy with the king of clubs in order to take the 'marked' finesse of the nine of diamonds. His innocent faith was shattered when West produced the ten of diamonds and cashed four spade tricks to put the contract one down.

South is entitled to a measure of sympathy. A less enterprising declarer, seeing no point in testing the diamonds, would simply have taken the heart finesse and made his contract. South's efforts to find an alternative to the heart finesse, while worthy, were a little transparent, and West, who knew that the heart finesse was working, seized the opportunity to put the boot in. This is the essence of deceptive defense, to take your chances as they come along.

There are many hands where the declarer has several chances for his contract and will probably succeed if allowed to test the possibilities in logical order. It is up to the defenders to make things difficult for him, switching the signposts in an effort to persuade declarer to take the wrong turning.

See what happened on the following hand.

```
                    ♠ 8 3 2
                    ♡ 9 7 4
                    ◇ A K 8 4 2
                    ♣ A 7
  ♠ Q 10 7 5 4                    ♠ J 9 6
  ♡ J 10 6 3                      ♡ Q 8 2
  ◇ 3                             ◇ Q J 10 5
  ♣ J 9 2                         ♣ K 10 6
                    ♠ A K
                    ♡ A K 5
                    ◇ 9 7 6
                    ♣ Q 8 5 4 3
```

Both vulnerable.   **South**   **North**
Dealer South.   1NT   3NT

West led the five of spades to the jack and king, and the declarer paused to take stock of his prospects. With seven top tricks, he needed to develop two more in one of the minor suits, and he could only afford to lose the lead once in the process. He decided that the best plan was to start by playing off the ace and king of diamonds and shift to clubs if the diamonds broke badly.

As can be seen this plan succeeds, for although the diamonds are 4-1 the lie of the clubs is favorable. But something happened along the way to change South's mind and set him on the wrong road. When he played a diamond to dummy's king East dropped the ten!

This opened up for South the exciting possibility of making four diamond tricks not only when the suit broke 3-2 but also when East had a singleton, which looked quite probable. Accordingly, at the third trick South played a small diamond from the table. Disillusionment set in swiftly when East won and West discarded a heart. A spade came back, and it was too late for any attempt to establish the clubs. All South could do was concede another diamond to East and settle for one down.

It is good practice in defense to drop an honor card in fourth position whenever you can afford it. What is more, the higher the card the more effective it is likely to be. Consider this ordinary position.

              9 5 4

K Q 10 3   6 2
              A J 8 7

Looking for tricks in this suit, declarer runs the nine from dummy. If you win with the ten, South is likely to abandon the suit and try elsewhere, perhaps more successfully, for the tricks he needs. You should, of course, win with the queen or the king on the first round. South may then be encouraged to persevere with his hopeless suit.

Do you sympathise with declarer in a situation like this? Do you feel sorry for him when it is clear that he is going down in a hopeless contract? If so, it does you credit as a human being, but someone so lacking in killer instinct will never be a really tricky player. The toughest competitors may be the most charming and considerate people you could hope to meet in everyday life, but when they sit down at the bridge table they give and expect no quarter. Having got their man down, they look for ways of putting the boot in and stomping him into the ground.

It is one of the facts of competitive life that there can be no winners without losers, and your task at the bridge table is to win by as large a margin as possible. In the pairs game a near-top is better than an average-plus, and a complete top is better still. The fact that a complete top for you means a complete bottom for your opponent is something that has to be accepted. His misery is the price that has to be paid for your happiness.

A good, sadistic way of increasing your opponent's misery is to offer a glimmer of hope when he is playing in a hopeless contract. Here is an example.

```
                    ♠ 10 6 4
                    ♥ K 5
                    ♦ J 9 3
 ♠ A K Q 9 5 2      ♣ K Q J 7 2      ♠ J 3
 ♥ Q J 10 6                          ♥ 4 2
 ♦ 5                                 ♦ 10 8 6 2
 ♣ A 4              ♠ 8 7            ♣ 10 9 8 6 5
                    ♥ A 9 8 7 3
                    ♦ A K Q 7 4
                    ♣ 3
```

Match-point pairs.
Neither vulnerable.
Dealer South.

South	West	North	East
1 ♡	2 ♠	Double	Pass
3 ◇	Pass	3 ♡	Pass
Pass	Double	Pass	Pass
Pass			

You start with top spades, partner discarding a club on the third round and South ruffing. When the three of clubs is played you go up with the ace and shift to the queen of hearts. Declarer wins on the table with the king and plays another heart to his ace, and you should have the ten of hearts all ready to drop.

If you play the six of hearts under the ace, nothing is more sure than that South will abandon trumps and play on the minors for one off. This may not be good enough, for some may be allowed to make three spades on your cards.

In the pause that follows your play of the ten of hearts on the second round you can almost hear South thinking: 'Has this idiot on my left doubled with only three trumps? If so, I can make the contract.' If South *does* continue with the nine of hearts his cup of misery will overflow, for you will force him with spades to extract a penalty of 500.

Declarers will often clutch at straws in attempting to save a sinking contract. On the next hand a declarer held out a substantial straw, then stepped back and watched declarer drown.

```
              ♠ J 10 3
              ♡ A K 7
              ◇ K Q 10 5
              ♣ 8 7 3
♠ A 9 5 4                        ♠ Q 8 7 2
♡ Q 10 5                         ♡ 8 6 3
◇ A 4                            ◇ 9 6 2
♣ K 10 9 2                       ♣ 6 5 4
              ♠ K 6
              ♡ J 9 4 2
              ◇ J 8 7 3
              ♣ A Q J
```

Match-point pairs.
Both vulnerable.
Dealer West.

West	North	East	South
1♣	Pass	Pass	1NT
Pass	3NT	Pass	Pass
Pass			

West led the four of spades and East did the right thing by playing the eight under dummy's jack. Declarer played a diamond to the jack and ace, and after cashing the ace of spades, dropping the king, West continued with the nine of spades to the ten and queen. Declarer discarded a diamond on the third spade and another diamond on the fourth spade as dummy threw a club. East then shifted to a club and South won despairingly with the ace.

Entering dummy with his remaining diamond, South cashed the ace of hearts. If nothing exciting happened he intended next to concede a club. This would enable him to escape for one off, since West was

marked with the queen of hearts and would have to
concede the rest of the tricks on his return.

But West was not a player to be satisfied with 100
when 200 might be available. He made sure that
something exciting *did* happen by dropping the ten of
hearts under the ace. To South this looked like a possible reprieve, for if West had Q 10 doubleton in hearts
the contract could be made after all. Unable to resist
the bait, he continued with the king of hearts and was
shortly writing minus 200 on the score-sheet.

Another way of adding to declarer's misery is to offer
him an inducement to take a losing finesse.

```
                    ♠ A J 10
                    ♡ K J
                    ◇ A J 9 5 3
                    ♣ 10 7 6
 ♠ 9 7 6 2                            ♠ K 8 4
 ♡ Q 9 8 6 3                         ♡ A 7 2
 ◇ 6 4                               ◇ Q 10 8
 ♣ 8 4                               ♣ Q J 9 3
                    ♠ Q 5 3
                    ♡ 10 5 4
                    ◇ K 7 2
                    ♣ A K 5 2
```

Match-point pairs.

North-South vulnerable.
Dealer South.

South	West	North	East
Pass	Pass	1◇	Pass
2NT	Pass	3NT	Pass
Pass	Pass		

West led the six of hearts to the jack and ace. East returned the seven of hearts on which West played the

three. At this point East knew that the heart suit was ready to run as soon as he gained the lead. Declarer was known to have one heart left which could not be the queen, since West would not have led the fourth-highest card from 10 9 8 6 3.

South played a diamond to his king and finessed the jack of diamonds on the way back, losing to the queen. Giving no thought to a heart return (who's interested in one off?), East shifted to the queen of clubs. Now it looked to South as though East had started with only two hearts. In that case the spade finesse would be completely safe, worth ten tricks if it succeeded and nine if it failed.

In practice it proved to be worth only seven tricks, and South made a mental note never to trust East again.

Chapter 11

DECEIVING THE EXPERTS

The time has come to take a look at some of the more subtle ways of leading defenders astray. Delicate forms of deception tend to work best against thinking opponents, and much will depend on your estimate of the caliber of the opposition on any particular hand. There is little point in taking a great deal of trouble to induce a miscount if your opponent is quite incapable of counting the hand. Nor can it be sensible to project an illusion with delicate brush-strokes in front of the eyes of a defender who lacks the imagination to appreciate its significance. Choose your weapons to suit the occasion. The better your opponents the more willing you should be to exchange the bludgeon for the rapier.

K J 6 5

7 3

Suppose that your contract depends on a correct guess in this suit. It was suggested in an earlier chapter that you should put West to an immediate test by playing the suit from hand at trick two. Unsure of the position at this early stage, West may be rattled into going up with the ace if he has it.

This is good general advice, but against counting opponents there will sometimes be a better way of putting West under pressure. Consider the following hand.

```
          ♠ 10 5 3
          ♡ K Q 5
          ◇ K J 7 6 4
          ♣ A 6
♠ Q 9 8 6 4              ♠ K J 7 2
♡ 8 3                    ♡ 7 6
◇ A 9 2                  ◇ Q 10 5
♣ 10 4 2                 ♣ 9 8 5 3
          ♠ A
          ♡ A J 10 9 4 2
          ◇ 8 3
          ♣ K Q J 7
```

Match-point pairs.
Both vulnerable.
Dealer North.

North	South
1 ◇	1 ♡
2 ♡	4NT
5 ◇	6 ♡

West leads the six of spades to the king and ace. You have eleven top tricks and must look to the diamonds for the twelfth. Clearly there is a lot to be said for playing a diamond at trick two. However, if the trumps break evenly, it should be possible to convince West that you have a singleton diamond, in which case he will certainly take the ace if he has it for fear of allowing you to make all thirteen tricks.

The right move is to draw the trumps and then play four rounds of clubs, discarding the two remaining spades from the table. If West is persuaded that you started with a 2-6-1-4 distribution, he is sure to shoot up with the ace on your next play of a diamond.

The technique in such situations is to trade on your opponent's ignorance of the true position and project a plausible alternative in his mind. Fortunately in the above case East was unable to indicate his distribution, and West could not arrive at the right answer by asking himself why you had played in this manner. If you really had a 2-6-1-4 shape you would have no choice but to dispose of the spade losers before tackling the diamonds.

If the right illusion is built up, a finesse may be allowed to succeed even when it is wrong.

```
                    ♠ A Q
                    ♡ K J 10 4
                    ◊ 9 7 3
                    ♣ A J 10 3
  ♠ J 10 9 2                        ♠ 8 4 3
  ♡ 7 2                             ♡ 5
  ◊ A J 6                           ◊ Q 8 5 4 2
  ♣ K 7 5 4                         ♣ Q 9 6 2
                    ♠ K 7 6 5
                    ♡ A Q 9 8 6 3
                    ◊ K 10
                    ♣ 8
```

Neither vulnerable.
Dealer South.

South	North
1♡	3♣
3♡	4♡
4NT	5♡
6♡	Pass

West leads the jack of spades to dummy's queen, and you see that your main hope must be to find the ace of diamonds with East. There is the additional chance that the king and queen of clubs will come down in three rounds, of course, so you cash the ace of clubs at trick two and continue with a club ruff. No honor appears and you have to fall back on the diamonds.

However, you have trumps to spare and it cannot hurt to complete the elimination of the clubs. You enter dummy with the ten of hearts, ruff another club with the eight of hearts, and return to the jack of hearts, East discarding a diamond. When you ruff the last club with the ace of hearts you have reached the following position:

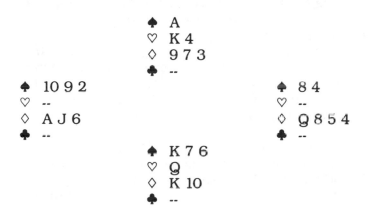

One card in your hand is completely superfluous-- the king of spades. It must therefore be right at this point to lead the king of spades to dummy's ace in the hope of inducing a miscount. When you continue with a diamond to your king West may allow it to win, believing this to be the position:

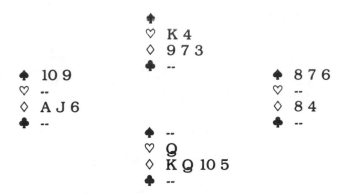

♠
♥ K 4
♦ 9 7 3
♣ --

♠ 10 9   ♠ 8 7 6
♥ --   ♥ --
♦ A J 6   ♦ 8 4
♣ --   ♣ --

♠ --
♥ Q
♦ K Q 10 5
♣ --

In the above diagram it would be a fatal mistake for West to take his ace for he would then be end-played, forced to yield the twelfth trick whether he returned a diamond or a spade.

To be sure, West may avoid the trap if he asks himself why his partner should discard a diamond from three cards rather than a spade from five. But even the most imaginative defender may fail to look so deeply into the position or fail to reach the right conclusion if he does.

While looking for opportunities to induce a miscount, you must keep up your guard at all times, for the defenders may be trying to give you the same treatment. Try the next hand as a single-dummy problem.

♠ 7 4
♥ A 10 6 4 3 2
♦ 6
♣ K 10 4 3

♠ A 10 6 2
♥ J 7
♦ Q J 10 7 3
♣ A 6

Neither vulnerable.
Dealer South.

South	West	North	East
1NT	Pass	2 ◇	Pass
2 ♡	Pass	Pass	Pass

After a dubious weak notrump opening and a transfer response, you become declarer in two hearts and
West leads the king of spades.

You hold off, and West continues with the queen of
spades to your ace. The queen of diamonds runs to
East's king at trick three. After ruffing the spade return in dummy, you play a club to your ace, ruff a diamond on the table and cash the king of clubs. West
drops the jack, which looks ominous, but you ruff the
next club with the seven of hearts anyway. West over-
ruffs with the nine of hearts and plays the jack of
spades.

Not wanting to suffer another over-ruff, you discard
the ten of clubs from dummy. East also discards a club
and West now plays a small diamond. When you ruff
on the table the ace comes down from East. How
should you continue?

At this point you have ♡ A 10 6 left in dummy opposite ♡ J and ◇ J 10 in your own hand. A complete
count on the hand is available. East apparently started
with three spades, three diamonds, five clubs and
therefore two hearts, and it is just a matter of playing
the ace and another trump to make your contract.

But when you think about it more closely there is
something that does not quite add up. If East really
started with K 8 or Q 8 in trumps, why did he not discard his ace of diamonds on the fourth spade? He
could then have made sure of defeating the contract by
over-ruffing when his partner's diamond shift was
ruffed in dummy. This is not a difficult play for a re-

sourceful defender, and it begins to look as though East must have dropped the ace of diamonds in order to induce a miscount on your part.

Naturally you have no intention of letting him get away with that. You should continue with a low heart from the table, expecting the complete deal to be:

```
                    ♠ 7 4
                    ♡ A 10 6 4 3 2
                    ◇ 6
                    ♣ K 10 4 3
   ♠ K Q J 8                        ♠ 9 5 3
   ♡ K Q 9 5                        ♡ 8
   ◇ 9 4 2                          ◇ A K 8 5
   ♣ J 5                            ♣ Q 9 8 7 2
                    ♠ A 10 6 2
                    ♡ J 7
                    ◇ Q J 10 7 3
                    ♣ A 6
```

East's singleton trump could equally well be the queen or the king. Dropping the ace of diamonds on the third round was a cunning move which could have taken in a counting declarer who did not bother to think his problem through.

The next hand comes from the Camrose International between Scotland and England in 1981.

```
                    ♠ Q 3
                    ♡ J 5 2
                    ◇ Q 9 7 3
                    ♣ J 9 5 2
   ♠ A 8 7 4 2                      ♠ K 6 5
   ♡ 9 7                            ♡ 10 8 3
   ◇ 6 4                            ◇ A J 10 8 2
   ♣ 10 8 6 4                       ♣ A 7
                    ♠ J 10 9
                    ♡ A K Q 6 4
                    ◇ K 5
                    ♣ K Q 3
```

North-South vulnerable.
Dealer East.

West	North	East	South
		1NT	Double
2♠	Double	Pass	4♡
Pass	Pass	Pass	

The double of two spades purported to show values, but when West led the six of diamonds and dummy went down, the declarer, Barnet Shenkin of Scotland, must have been disappointed to see that the 'values' consisted of two queens and two jacks.

The defenders were in a position to cash four fast tricks, but no contract is hopeless until it has actually gone down. East put in the eight of diamonds, allowing the king to win the first trick, and Shenkin played the king of clubs. When this held he continued with the queen of clubs.

In with the club ace, East had a difficult decision to make. Now the point of playing clubs before touching trumps can be seen. If East had known that South had solid trumps, he would have no option but to play a spade in the hope of finding his partner with the ace. As it was, East could hope for his partner to have an honor in trumps instead of the spade ace, in which case the defenders might be able to organise a ruff in both minor suits.

After considerable thought, East cashed the ace of diamonds and continued with the two, and that was all the help that Shenkin needed. He ruffed the third diamond with the ace of hearts, drew trumps with the jack, queen and king, and played a club for a finesse of the nine. One spade went away on the club jack and another on the queen of diamonds, giving declarer ten well-earned tricks.

The same ambitious contract was reached in the other room, but the defense started off on a different tack. West led a club to his partner's ace and East returned the suit. Having unblocked his queen on the first round, declarer won the second club in dummy, played a diamond to his king, drew two rounds of trumps with the ace and king, and played his third club.

Declarer would have succeeded if the clubs had been 3-3 or if East had been out of trumps, for he would have been able to discard his diamond loser on the fourth club. As it was, East ruffed the third club, cashed the ace of diamonds, and then played a spade to put the contract two down.

At times it can pay to leave a defender in no doubt whatever about your shape as long as a lingering doubt remains about your high card strength. The declarer was lucky on the following hand to have on his left an imaginative player who was strong enough to be deceived.

```
                    ♠ A 9 7 3
                    ♡ 10 7 5 4
                    ◇ A K 8
                    ♣ 6 3
  ♠ 5                                ♠ J 2
  ♡ A K 6                            ♡ J 9 8 3
  ◇ J 7 2                            ◇ Q 10 9 6 5 3
  ♣ A Q J 8 7 4                      ♣ 10
                    ♠ K Q 10 8 6 4
                    ♡ Q 2
                    ◇ 4
                    ♣ K 9 5 2
```

Neither vulnerable.
Dealer South.

South	West	North	East
2♠ *	3♣	4♠	Pass
Pass	Pass		

6-10 points

West started with the king and ace of hearts. A shift to the ace and another club at this point would have settled the issue, but West continued reasonably enough with a third heart for South to ruff. It seemed only a temporary reprieve, since there was no obvious way of disposing of one of the club losers.

However, reasoning that West was likely to have a six-card club suit, West saw a slender technical chance and a rather larger psychological one. He decided to go hunting for one of the rarest creatures in the bridge jungle--the phantom crocodile.

After drawing trumps with the king and ace, South ruffed the fourth heart, played off the ace and king of diamonds for a club discard, and ruffed the third diamond. With everyone reduced to four cards, he played the five of clubs from hand in the following ending:

```
                    ♠ 9 7
                    ♡ --
                    ◇ --
                    ♣ 6 3
    ♠ --                           ♠ --
    ♡ --                           ♡ --
    ◇ --                           ◇ Q 10 9
    ♣ A Q J 8                      ♣ 10
                    ♠ 10
                    ♡ --
                    ◇ --
                    ♣ K 9 5
```

By this time West had a complete count on the hand and knew that his partner had started with a singleton club. His problem revolved around the rank of this singleton. South did not need to have the king of clubs, which would make him top weight for his weak two bid. Indeed, it seemed to West that South might have chosen to open one spade if he had held the club king. It appeared to be more than likely that East's singleton would be the king, in which case he must not be allowed to win a trick with it, since he would have to concede a ruff and discard on his diamond return.

After much agonised thought, West came to the conclusion that it was his duty to play the ace of clubs on declarer's five, opening his jaws wide like the crocodile to swallow his partner's supposed king. All there was to swallow in reality was the bitter knowledge that he had allowed an impossible game to make.

South's legitimate chance? If East's singleton had been the queen, there would have been no defense after the third round of hearts.

That was a complicated hand, but sometimes the most subtle of deceptive plays is simplicity itself. This famous coup by the late, great Howard Schenken is worth another look.

```
              ♠ J 10 8 6 4
              ♡ 7 6
              ◇ 9 7 2
              ♣ 6 3 2
♠ --                        ♠ A 5 3 2
♡ J 8 4 3                   ♡ K Q 10 9
◇ K 10 8 6 4                ◇ J 5
♣ K J 8 7                   ♣ Q 9 4
              ♠ K Q 9 7
              ♡ A 5 2
              ◇ A Q 3
              ♣ A 10 5
```

Both vulnerable.
Dealer East.

West	North	East	South
		1 ♠	1NT
2 ◇	Pass	Pass	2NT
Pass	Pass	Pass	

The bidding is explained by the fact that it was rub-
ber bridge and North-South had 60 towards their second game. West led the six of diamonds to the jack and
queen.

This was a good start for Schenken but he could see
problems ahead. There were just four quick winners,
and only three more could be developed in spades.
Why not four? Well, East, a fellow expert, had bid
spades and would certainly hold up his ace until the
fourth round in order to shut out dummy. Was there
any way round the problem?

Howard Schenken's solution was simple and ele-
gant. At trick two he returned the three of diamonds.
Naturally West was delighted to be given the chance of
establishing his suit. He won the ten of diamonds and
played another round to knock out the ace. Equally
naturally, East discarded one of his 'useless' small
spades on the third diamond.

All had gone according to Schenken's master plan.
On winning the ace of diamonds he quickly knocked
out the ace of spades and claimed his eight tricks.

One the trickiest of the world's great players, Gabriel
Chagas of Brazil, is well versed in the delicate art of
manipulating his opponents. Watch him at work on
this hand from the match between Brazil and Israel in
the 1980 World Team Olympiad.

```
              ♠ 6
              ♡ K J 7
              ◊ 4 2
              ♣ A 10 8 7 5 4 2
♠ A 10 7 4                      ♠ Q 9 5 2
♡ A 8 4                         ♡ 5 3
◊ Q 10 8                        ◊ J 9 6 5 3
♣ K 9 3         ♠ K J 8 3      ♣ Q 6
                ♡ Q 10 9 6 2
                ◊ A K 7
                ♣ J
```

East-West vulnerable.
Dealer North.

West	North	East	South
	Pass	Pass	1♣ *
Pass	2♣ **	Pass	2♡
Pass	3♣ ***	Pass	4♡
Pass	Pass	Pass	

*Olympic Club
**Positive with clubs
***Promising heart support

West led the four of hearts and dummy's seven won
the trick. Chagas took some time to consider his problems, which were many since West had clearly found a
killing lead. If he played a spade at trick two, the
defenders would certainly continue with two more
rounds of trumps, holding him to eight tricks. A ninth
trick could always be made by ruffing a diamond before tackling the spades, but Chagas had little interest
in making nine tricks.

The one thing in his favor was that East could not be
aware of the true trump position. If East could be persuaded that he, Chagas, had the ace of hearts and was
hoping to establish the club suit, he might shift to
spades himself in an attempt to kill dummy. This
seemed the best hope, so Chagas played a diamond to

his king and then ran the jack of clubs to East's queen.

East can hardly be blamed for taking the bait. It looked as though it might be imperative to force dummy to ruff in order to shut out the club suit, and East shifted at trick four to the queen of spades. Chagas made the second key play when he ducked in hand. Convinced that he had declarer on the run, East continued with a spade to the king and ace. Declarer ruffed in dummy, returned to hand with the ace of diamonds, cashed the jack of spades, and ruffed his third diamond on the table. The ace of clubs provided a parking place for the fourth spade, and the only other trick for the defense was the ace of trumps.

It takes something special to bring home dubious games of this sort. The declarer's play provides a valuable object lesson in how to tackle an impossible contract. Naturally both defenders could have done better --East by continuing the trump attack, and West, who knew more about the position, by overtaking his partner's queen of spades and playing the ace and another heart. But neither play was easy to see through the smoke-screen laid down by Chagas.

Subtle play is sometimes needed in order to conceal from the defenders your ultimate aim of obtaining discards in dummy. Consider this hand.

```
                    ♠ Q 10 7 6 3
                    ♡ A 8 6 4
                    ◇ J 9 3
 ♠ 4                ♣ 5              ♠ 9 2
 ♡ Q J 10 5                          ♡ K 9 7 2
 ◇ A Q 6                             ◇ K 8 5 4
 ♣ A J 10 7 2                        ♣ 8 6 3
                    ♠ A K J 8 5
                    ♡ 3
                    ◇ 10 7 2
                    ♣ K Q 9 4
```

East-West vulnerable.
Dealer South.

South	West	North	East
1 ♠	Double	4 ♠	Pass
Pass	Pass		

West leads the queen of hearts to dummy's ace, and you note ruefully that there are four top losers. East apparently has the king of hearts, and he must have one of the top diamonds as well since West did not lead the suit. This means that the ace of clubs is bound to be with West.

The trouble with playing a club to your king or queen at trick two is that West is likely to spot the danger of a discard from dummy and shift to diamonds, putting you down straight away.

You must try to convince West that your club holding represents no threat to the defense, and the best way of doing that is by playing a club to your nine at trick two. Now West may fail to appreciate the urgent need to cash out and may continue with a second heart. After drawing trumps and ruffing out the ace of clubs, you will then be able to dispose of one of the diamond losers on the established club.

On the next hand the declarer's play can hardly be described as subtle, but it certainly proved effective against a defender who was not fully awake.

```
                    ♠ K 6 3
                    ♡ 10 4
                    ◇ A Q J 3
      ♠ A 8 5       ♣ 7 6 5 2
      ♡ 8 6 5 3                    ♠ 7 2
      ◇ 10 7 2                     ♡ A Q J 2
      ♣ Q J 4                      ◇ 9 5
                    ♠ Q J 10 9 4   ♣ A K 10 8 3
                    ♡ K 9 7
                    ◇ K 8 6 4
                    ♣ 9
```

Both vulnerable.
Dealer East.

West	North	East	South
		1♣	1♠
2♣	4♠	Pass	Pass
Pass			

West led the queen of clubs, and East played well by overtaking with the king and returning the seven of spades. South and West played low and the king won the trick. When the four of hearts was played from the table, East again did the right thing by putting in the queen. If he had won with the ace and continued the spade attack, he would eventually have been squeezed in hearts and clubs.

After winning the heart king South returned the seven of hearts to the ten and jack. East led his second spade and West played the ace and another, removing the last trump from dummy. Denied the opportunity to ruff a heart, South went for the one slender chance that was left. He played the six of diamonds to dummy's jack, ruffed a club in hand, played the eight of diamonds to the queen, and ruffed another club with his last trump. He then played the king of diamonds and overtook with the ace, leaving this two-card ending:

```
                ♠  --
                ♡  --
                ◇  3
                ♣  7
♠  --                        ♠  --
♡  8 6                       ♡  A
◇  --                        ◇  --
♣  --                        ♣  10
                ♠  --
                ♡  9
                ◇  4
                ♣  --
```

East had been so busy congratulating himself on his fine defense that he had failed to take proper note of the diamond spots. When the diamond three was played from the table he was jerked back to attention. Who had the master diamond? East was vaguely aware that South had been doing some unblocking in the suit. It seemed probable that South had concealed the two, hoping to score dummy's club at the end. Besides, West might have the nine of hearts. Reasoning on those lines, East parted with the ace of hearts and another impossible game rolled home.

It is perhaps inappropriate to refer to the above ending as a pseudo-squeeze, although it certainly felt like a squeeze to East who could not remember whether the three of diamonds was high or not.

The more normal form of pseudo-squeeze has a big role to play in the deceptive strategy of the declarer. Even when there is no genuine play for the contract, it is worth while trying the effect of playing off the trumps or the long suit. Surprising things can happen when a defender imagines himself to be squeezed.

One of the most brilliant swindles on record was perpetrated by the late M. Harrison Gray in the 1966 European Championships at Warsaw.

```
              ♠ 9 7 2
              ♡ J 3
              ◇ K Q 9 3
              ♣ A 10 7 2
♠ J 8 6 3                      ♠ Q 5
♡ K 10 8 7                     ♡ 9 6 4 2
◇ J 10 4 2                     ◇ A 7 6 5
♣ 3                            ♣ J 9 6
              ♠ A K 10 4
              ♡ A Q 5
              ◇ 8
              ♣ K Q 8 5 4
```

East-West vulnerable.
Dealer South.

Pressing for sorely needed points in the match between Britain and Norway, Gray and Priday bid to six
clubs on a sequence that is best forgotten. It is clearly
an impossible contract, but Gray had bid diamonds to
inhibit the lead and was duly rewarded when West led
a heart.

Winning with the jack, Gray entered his hand with a
trump and led his diamond, hoping to find the ace
with West. His luck had run out. East captured the
queen of diamonds with the ace, and there appeared to
be no way for declarer to avoid the loss of a spade trick.

But Gray was never one to concede defeat. He won
the heart return with the ace, ruffed his third heart in
dummy and played out all the trumps, leaving the
king of diamonds high and dry on the table. It was
hard for West to believe that Gray had cut himself off
from the master diamond, and he discarded two
spades in order to keep the jack and ten of diamonds.
You can imagine his chagrin when Gray proceeded to
make four spade tricks and his slam.

Chapter 12

SUBTLE DEFENSE

For the defenders, just as for declarer, the degree of deception employed should be tailored to match the standard of the opposition. Subtle false cards are wasted against an unimaginative declarer, who will just continue to play the cards in front of his nose regardless of your best efforts. It is the strong and imaginative declarers who are most easily deceived by subtle methods. Consider this ordinary card combination:

$$\begin{array}{ccc} & \text{J 10 7 3 2} & \\ \text{K Q 8 4} & & \text{9 5} \\ & \text{A 6} & \end{array}$$

Needing to develop tricks in a notrump contract, declarer plays the ace followed by the six. If South is a weak player the defenders have no chance of making more than two tricks, and West may as well play the queen on the second round. But if South is a strong player who knows his percentages, West can secure a third trick for the defense by playing the eight on the second round. Declarer will play low from dummy, the correct percentage play to cater for a doubleton honor in the East hand.

One thing the defenders can be sure about when facing strong opposition is that the declarer will make a determined effort to count their hands. It is up to the defenders to take protective measures.

Concealing the thirteenth card in a suit may be all that is needed to point declarer in the wrong direction.

```
                ♠ K 7 4
                ♡ Q 8 3
                ◇ Q 4
                ♣ K 9 8 5 2
  ♠ A 9 3                          ♠ 10 8 6 2
  ♡ J 10 9 5                       ♡ K 7 2
  ◇ J 6                            ◇ 9 8 5 3
  ♣ Q 10 7 3                       ♣ J 6
                ♠ Q J 5
                ♡ A 6 4
                ◇ A K 10 7 2
                ♣ A 4
```

Neither vulnerable.
Dealer South.

South	North
1 ◇	2 ♣
3NT	Pass

West led the jack of hearts to the three, seven and
ace. At trick two declarer played the queen of spades,
and West won immediately in order to continue with
the ten of hearts. This was covered by the queen and
king, and East returned the two of hearts to the nine.

Seeing little hope of a fifth defensive trick if he
cashed the last heart, West tried the effect of shifting
back to spades. Declarer won with the jack and considered the position. He had eight top tricks and the contract seemed to be safe if he could develop the diamonds without giving the lead to East, who apparently
had the thirteenth heart. Accordingly, after a diamond
to the queen, South finessed the ten of diamonds on
the way back. West won with the jack and produced
the thirteenth heart as the setting trick.

Clearly if West had cashed his fourth heart at an earlier stage, South would have had to rely, successfully,
on dropping the jack of diamonds in three rounds.

```
              ♠ A 10 8 5
              ♡ K Q 6
              ◊ 8 3
              ♣ K 8 5 4
♠ Q 6 3                        ♠ 4
♡ J 9 7 3                      ♡ A 10 8 4
◊ Q 10 5                       ◊ 9 7 6 2
♣ 10 6 2                       ♣ A J 9 3
              ♠ K J 9 7 2
              ♡ 5 2
              ◊ A K J 4
              ♣ Q 7
```

Match-point pairs.

Both vulnerable.

Dealer South.

South	North
1♠	3♠
4♠	Pass

The three of hearts is led to the queen and ace, and a heart is returned to dummy's king. Declarer plays a low club to his queen and continues with a second club to the eight and nine. The diamond shift goes to the king, and after cashing the ace of diamonds declarer continues with the four, ruffing West's queen in dummy. Next comes the five of clubs.

While all this is going on East should have been asking himself why declarer is messing about in the side suits instead of drawing trumps. The answer can only be that he has a two-way guess in trumps and is looking to the fall of the cards in the other suits to provide a clue to the trump distribution. He already knows that East has four hearts and will assume that he has four diamonds. If he discovers that East has four clubs as well, he will have no further problems. After cashing the king of spades he will finesse against West to make an overtrick.

If East has worked this out in good time, he will have the ace of clubs ready to play on the third round. This may persuade South to hold himself to ten tricks by playing for 2-2 trumps.

A declarer was persuaded to adopt a losing line of play on this hand from the British Trials of 1975.

```
                    ♠ A K 3
                    ♡ A K 8 4
                    ◇ K 6 4
♠ J 6               ♣ A Q 5            ♠ 9 7 4
♡ 10 7 2                               ♡ Q 9 5
◇ A J 10 9                             ◇ 8 7 3
♣ 8 6 3 2           ♠ Q 10 8 5 2       ♣ K J 9 7
                    ♡ J 6 3
                    ◇ Q 5 2
                    ♣ 10 4
```

Neither vulnerable.
Dealer North.

	North	South
	2♣	2◇
	2NT	3♠
	4♠	Pass

Three notrumps would have been easy, but South played in four spades and received an unfriendly lead of the six of clubs. East was allowed to win with the jack, and the eight of diamonds was returned to the queen and ace. A second club went to the queen and king, and a diamond was returned to dummy's king.

At this point the correct technical play (and the winning line) is to draw two rounds of trumps with the ace and queen and then test the hearts. When the queen fails to drop, declarer discards the jack of hearts on the club ace and ruffs a heart in hand. Dummy is entered with the king of spades, and the losing diamond goes away on the established heart.

No doubt declarer intended to play that way, but a funny thing happened when he played the ace of spades: the jack dropped on his left! That put a different complexion on the hand. If East had four trumps, the only chance of making the contract lay in a red-suit squeeze against West. Accordingly, South discarded his diamond on the ace of clubs and continued with the king and another trump. On the lie of the cards he then had to go one down.

Sometimes the information declarer needs concerns your quota of high cards rather than your distribution. Defenders must guard their secrets jealously in cases like the following.

```
                    ♠ A Q J
                    ♡ J 10 4
                    ◊ 9 5 2
♠ 10 8 4 3          ♣ Q J 6 5          ♠ K 9 2
♡ K                                    ♡ 8 2
◊ K J 10 4                             ◊ 8 7 6 3
♣ 10 8 7 2          ♠ 7 6 5            ♣ A K 9 4
                    ♡ A Q 9 7 6 5 3
                    ◊ A Q
                    ♣ 3
```

Neither vulnerable.
Dealer North.

West	North	East	South
	Pass	Pass	1 ♡
Pass	2 ♣ *	Pass	4 ♡
Pass	Pass	Pass	

Drury

West leads the three of spades to the jack and king. East returns a diamond to the queen and king, and West continues with the jack of diamonds to the ace.

South now plays the three of clubs to the eight, jack and king.

Declarer has been unlucky with his finesses so far. Is he going to be unlucky with the trump finesse as well? It depends on East, who has all the information he needs to make an intelligent decision. South's club play is a clear indication that he is trying to discover the lie of the honors in the side suits before committing himself to a decision in trumps, and East knows from his partner's eight that there is only one club trick for the defense. He must therefore conceal the true position by returning the four of clubs.

South will ruff and, believing the ace of clubs to be with West, will see no reason to refuse the trump finesse. If East had made it plain that he held both top clubs (either by trying to cash the ace or by shifting), South would know the location of the king of hearts. East would not have passed originally with 13 points, so South would play the ace of hearts on the first round, dropping the singleton king and making his contract.

Protecting singleton kings is one of the most vital arts of defense. Here is a further example.

```
                    ♠ A 5
                    ♡ 8 4
                    ◇ A Q J 8 5 3
                    ♣ Q 8 2
♠ K Q J 9                               ♠ 8 6 4 2
♡ 9 5 3                                 ♡ Q 10 7 6
◇ 7 6 4                                 ◇ K
♣ A 10 6                                ♣ J 7 4 3
                    ♠ 10 7 3
                    ♡ A K J 2
                    ◇ 10 9 2
                    ♣ K 9 5
```

Neither vulnerable.
Dealer West.

West	North	East	South
Pass	1 ◊	Pass	1 ♡
Pass	2 ◊	Pass	2NT
Pass	3NT	Pass	Pass
Pass			

You lead the king of spades to dummy's ace, East following with the six and South with the three. Declarer plays the two of clubs to his king, and unless you play low without a tremor you will have given away the game.

The key suit here is diamonds. If declarer has the king of diamonds you ,will defeat the contract only when partner has the heart ace. But if East has the diamond king it may well be bare, and there is no way that South will finesse in diamonds if you admit to the ace of clubs. He heard you pass originally.

When you play low at trick two, declarer is likely to go with the odds and finesse in diamonds, and after collecting your spades you can take the ace of clubs as the setting trick.

Anti-discovery play should be employed whenever you judge that declarer is trying to facilitate a subsequent guess.

```
                    ♠ Q 4 2
                    ♡ K 9 7 2
                    ◊ 8 3
♠ 10 9 5            ♣ A Q J 7          ♠ A K J 8 3
♡ 6                                    ♡ J 4
◊ A 10 7 5                             ◊ Q 9 4
♣ 10 8 6 5 2       ♠ 7 6              ♣ K 9 3
                    ♡ A Q 10 8 5 3
                    ◊ K J 6 2
                    ♣ 4
```

Both vulnerable.
Dealer East.

West	North	East	South
		1♠	2♡
2♠	4♡	Pass	Pass
Pass			

The defenders attacked in spades, declarer ruffing the third round. After cashing the ace of hearts, South played a club to the ace and returned the queen of clubs. Reasoning that a discard on clubs could not possibly help declarer, East calmly played low. South ruffed in hand, for he was not interested in discards but was merely seeking information. Convinced that the king of clubs was in the West hand, South decided that East must have the ace of diamonds for his opening bid. After a heart to the king, therefore, he played a diamond to his king and went down.

Clearly if East had covered the queen of clubs he would have surrendered valuable information to the enemy. South would then have taken the right view in diamonds, reasoning that West must have the ace to account for his raise to two spades.

A good way of preventing declarer from discovering what he needs to know about the hand is to attack an option at an early stage. I am indebted to Jean-Marc Roudinesco for the following deal.

```
                    ♠ 9 5
                    ♡ A Q J 10
                    ◇ A Q 10
                    ♣ K Q J 5
♠ K Q 10 7 6 4                    ♠ 3 2
♡ K 9                             ♡ 8 6 4 2
◇ J 9 6 2                         ◇ 5 4 3
♣ 2                              ♣ A 8 7 6
                    ♠ A J 8
                    ♡ 7 5 3
                    ◇ K 8 7
                    ♣ 10 9 4 3
```

North-South vulnerable.
Dealer North.

West	North	East	South
	1♣	Pass	1NT
2♠	3♠	Pass	3NT
Pass	Pass	Pass	

West leads the king of spades which draws the five, the two and the eight. Looking at all four hands, you can see that the contract is unbeatable, for even if West manages to set up his spades he can never regain the lead to cash them. On a diamond shift, for instance, declarer will knock out the ace of clubs, win the second or third spade, and fall back upon the heart finesse for his contract.

The only factor favoring the defenders is that declarer does not yet know the location of the key cards. West can take advantage of this by shifting to the nine of hearts at trick two. Now declarer is on a pure guess. For all he knows the king of hearts may be with East and the ace of clubs with West, in which case the only way of making the contract is to rise with the ace of hearts and knock out the club ace while he still controls the spades. It is the old, old story. If you make declarer guess, he will guess wrong part of the time.

One of the trickiest defenders among the great players of the world is Jean Besse of Switzerland. Watch how he lured an expert declarer to his doom on the following hand.

```
                    ♠ A 5 2
                    ♡ K J 4
                    ◇ 9 8 2
  ♠ 8 7 4           ♣ A Q 4 3          ♠ K 6 3
  ♡ Q 9 6 3                            ♡ 10 8 7 5
  ◇ A K 6 4                            ◇ Q 10 7 5
  ♣ 8 5             ♠ Q J 10 9         ♣ 10 7
                    ♡ A 2
                    ◇ J 3
                    ♣ K J 9 6 2
```

Match-point pairs.

Both vulnerable.
Dealer North.

West	North	East	South
	1♣	Pass	1♠
Pass	1NT	Pass	3♣
Pass	3♠	Pass	4♠
Pass	Pass	Pass	

West attacked in diamonds and declarer had to ruff the third round. The queen of spades was led for a finesse, and in the East seat Jean Besse played low without batting an eye. He had worked out that the contract would be made without difficulty if he took his king. Moreover, the opponents had bid rather too well. Three notrumps was likely to be the popular contract and there was no guarantee that it would make. The declarers might well lose four diamonds and the king of spades. Even if three notrumps was made a number of times, four spades would score better. Besse decided that a decent match-point score would come his way only if four spades were to be defeated. Accordingly, when South repeated the spade finesse Besse again played low, leaving this ususual position:

```
                ♠ A
                ♡ K J 4
                ◊ --
                ♣ A Q 4 3
   ♠ 8                        ♠ K
   ♡ Q 9 6 3                  ♡ 10 8 7 5
   ◊ 6                        ◊ 10
   ♣ 8 5                      ♣ 10 7
                ♠ 10
                ♡ A 2
                ◊ --
                ♣ K J 9 6 2
```

Unaware that he was caught in a web of deceit, South felt on top of the world at this stage. He too knew that making four spades would give him an excellent score. Rather than rely on 3-3 trumps, he decided to protect himself against a 4-2 break by leaving the trumps alone and playing on clubs, allowing West to ruff when he pleased. South planned to ruff a diamond return in hand, cross to dummy with the king of hearts, draw the last trump with the ace, and enjoy the rest of the clubs.

Alas, it did not work out like that for South. West ruffed the third club as East discarded a diamond, and on the diamond return Besse produced the card he was least expected to hold--the king of spades--to defeat the contract.

Another good way of bamboozling an expert declarer is to make a show of creating an entry for partner by means of a spectacular unblock. This Harrison Gray defense has appeared in a number of anthologies but it is worth another showing.

```
                    ♠ 9
                    ♡ A Q 10
                    ♢ K J 9 8 5 2
                    ♣ 9 8 2
♠ 8 3                                ♠ K Q J 7 6 4 2
♡ 9 6 4 3                            ♡ 8 7 5 2
♢ A Q 3                              ♢ 7
♣ K J 5 4                            ♣ 6
                    ♠ A 10 5
                    ♡ K J
                    ♢ 10 6 4
                    ♣ A Q 10 7 3
```

North-South vulnerable.
Dealer North.

West	North	East	South
	1 ♢	3 ♠	3NT
Pass	Pass	Pass	

Gray led the eight of spades to his partner's jack, and South held up his ace until the third round. On a normal defense declarer would play a diamond to the king at trick four and continue the suit. He would graciously concede two diamonds as well as the two spades already lost, claiming the rest of the tricks for his contract. But a strange thing happened on the third round of spades. West discarded the ace of diamonds!

South was not at all pleased with this development, for he knew and respected Gray's defense. It seemed to South that Gray had cleverly unblocked the ace of diamonds from A x, making it impossible for him to develop the diamonds without allowing East to gain the lead. The only counter appeared to be to try for tricks in clubs instead. Accordingly, South entered dummy with a heart and ran the nine of clubs.

Gray won with the jack and followed his deception through by returning the three of diamonds. Declarer went up with the king and played another club. East showed out, and when West won with the king he was able to take the setting trick with the diamond queen.

You could travel a long way before coming across a better swindle than that.

Getting back to a more mundane level, it is worth noting that an expert declarer can invent ways of going down that are beyond the reach of the average player.

```
              ♠ 8 5 4
              ♡ J 7
              ◇ 9 6 3
♠ 3           ♣ K Q 8 6 2    ♠ A K 10 9 6 2
♡ 9 8 5 3 2                  ♡ Q 10 4
◇ J 10 7                     ◇ K 4
♣ J 9 7 3     ♠ Q J 7        ♣ 10 5
              ♡ A K 6
              ◇ A Q 8 5 2
              ♣ A 4
```

Both vulnerable,
Dealer East.

West	North	East	South
		1♠	Double
Pass	2♣	Pass	2NT
Pass	3NT	Pass	Pass
Pass			

When West led the three of spades East saw little hope for the defense. It seemed pointless to duck since West would never be able to lead another spade. Nevertheless, East played the nine on the first trick, for he realised that the declarer would be unable to tell who had the two of spades.

On winning the trick South was far from happy about the situation. The diamond finesse was sure to be right, but he did not wish to bank on a 3-3 club break. It looked as though the defenders had maintained communication in spades, in which case they would be able to run four spade tricks when he gave up a trick in diamonds.

South therefore decided to 'cut communications' by returning a spade at trick two. This left him with only eight tricks and a red face.

It is easy to laugh at South's performance, but his play would have worked if East had held a spade fewer and a heart more. West would subsequently have been squeezed in the minor suits.

An artistic defense by Gabriel Chagas of Brazil was nominated for the brilliancy prize at the 1976 Olympiad.

```
                    ♠ Q 4
                    ♡ Q 9 2
                    ◇ A K J 8 4
                    ♣ J 9 3
  ♠ A K 8 2                          ♠ 10 9 6 5
  ♡ K 10 7                           ♡ A 4 3
  ◇ Q 10 7                           ◇ 5 3 2
  ♣ K 10 4                           ♣ 8 6 2
                    ♠ J 7 3
                    ♡ J 8 6 5
                    ◇ 9 6
                    ♣ A Q 7 5
```

Neither vulnerable.
Dealer North.

West	North	East	South
	1 ◇	Pass	1NT
Pass	Pass	Pass	

Chagas led the king of spades on which his partner,
Assumpcao, played the ten, indicating four cards in
the suit but denying the jack. Realising that the defense might have a chance if South could be prevented
from reaching his hand to take the diamond finesse,
Chagas continued with the two of spades to dummy's
queen.

When the jack of clubs was played at trick three
Chagas calmly dropped the ten, making it possible for
declarer to run the nine on the next round. South
might have smelt something fishy when Chagas
played the four under the nine, but he continued un-
suspectingly with a third club for a finesse of the
queen. Suddenly the roof fell in. Chagas won with the
king and played the ace and another spade, on which a
heart and a diamond were thrown from dummy. In
with the spade nine, Assumpcao played the ace and

another heart, and Chagas rounded off his sparkling defense by allowing dummy to win with the queen. Now declarer had to play diamonds from the table and the defenders finished with seven tricks--three spades, two hearts, a diamond and a club.

Sometimes the only hope for the defense lies in deceptive discarding.

```
                    ♠ K Q 7 4
                    ♡ 10 5
                    ◇ 7 5 4
                    ♣ A K 9 3
    ♠ 10 2                          ♠ J 9 6 5
    ♡ J 9 7 4 3                     ♡ K 2
    ◇ Q 10 9 6 3                    ◇ K J 2
    ♣ 6                             ♣ J 10 8 4
                    ♠ A 8 3
                    ♡ A Q 8 6
                    ◇ A 8
                    ♣ Q 7 5 2
```

Both vulnerable.
Dealer South.

South	North
1NT	2♣
2♡	3NT

West led the ten of diamonds and East put on the king. Declarer held up his ace but had to win when East continued with the jack of diamonds. South tested the clubs but had no luck in that suit, West discarding two small hearts. Next South played three rounds of spades. If the suit did not break he intended, according to West's discard, either to finesse in hearts or to throw West in with a diamond to enforce a heart return. But on the third round of spades West discarded the jack of hearts.

This caused some agonised thought on declarer's part. Had West started with six diamonds and K J x x in hearts and bared his king of hearts rather than submit to the end-play? It certainly looked dangerous to finesse in hearts now, but South saw that if West had started with six diamonds he could make sure of the contract whether West's remaining heart was the king or not. He played a heart to his ace and continued with a low heart, expecting that East would have to give him a further heart trick at the end. As the cards lay, of course, this was just about the only way to go down.

An expert may sometimes be persuaded to put a cold contract on the floor if a defender pretends to be squeezed.

```
                    ♠  A K 9 4
                    ♡  Q 10 7 3
                    ◇  A Q 4
                    ♣  8 5
  ♠  Q J 10 5                        ♠  8 6 3 2
  ♡  5 4                             ♡  A 2
  ◇  J 6 3                           ◇  9 7 2
  ♣  10 7 4 2                        ♣  K Q J 3
                    ♠  7
                    ♡  K J 9 8 6
                    ◇  K 10 8 5
                    ♣  A 9 6
```

East-West vulnerable.
Dealer South.

South	North
1♡	2♠
3◇	3♡
4♣	4◇
4NT	5♡
6♡	Pass

East prayed for a club lead but West was not tuned to the right wavelength and led the queen of spades to dummy's king. Declarer ruffed the four of spades in hand and played the king of hearts. East took his ace and shifted to the queen of clubs which was won by South's ace. After a heart to dummy's ten, South discarded a club on the ace of spades, ruffed the nine of spades in hand, played his last trump to the queen and cashed dummy's remaining trump.

Declarer fully intended to play for the drop in diamonds, but on the third and fourth rounds of hearts East discarded the jack and then the king of clubs. West also discarded two clubs, leaving this position:

```
              ♠  --
              ♡  --
              ◇  A Q 4
              ♣  8
♠  --                        ♠  --
♡  --                        ♡  --
◇  J 6 3                     ◇  9 7 2
♣  10                        ♣  3
              ♠  --
              ♡  --
              ◇  K 10 8 5
              ♣  --
```

It looked to South as though East had led the queen of clubs from K Q J in a clumsy attempt at deception but had subsequently been forced to throw his club honors in order to keep a four-card diamond holding. Accordingly, when both defenders followed with small diamonds under the ace and queen and East produced the nine on the third round, South put in the ten, losing the last two tricks to West.

East's stratagem of discarding all his high clubs was less dangerous than it looked. South was marked with the king of diamonds, and he was bound to make his contract anyway if he had the ten of clubs.

The aim of this type of defensive bluff may be to deter a finesse rather than to induce one, as the next hand shows.

```
                    ♠ 4
                    ♡ J 8 3
                    ♦ Q 9 8 5 3
                    ♣ A K 9 5
♠ 7                                      ♠ 10 9 6 3 2
♡ A K Q 10 7 6                           ♡ 9 2
♦ 6 4                                    ♦ K J 7 2
♣ J 8 4 3                                ♣ 10 6
                    ♠ A K Q J 8 5
                    ♡ 5 4
                    ♦ A 10
                    ♣ Q 7 2
```

North-South vulnerable.
Dealer South.

South	West	North	East
1 ♠	2 ♡	Double	Pass
4 ♠	Pass	Pass	Pass

West began with the king and ace of hearts. A diamond shift would have defeated the contract, but this was by no means obvious and in practice West continued with a third heart. East discarded a diamond and South ruffed.

Declarer tested the trumps, grimacing when West discarded a heart on the second round. Three more rounds of trumps were played, putting East on lead in the following position:

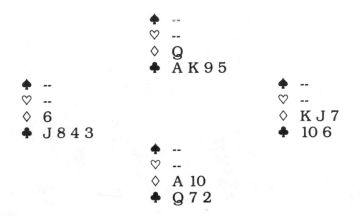

```
                 ♠  --
                 ♡  --
                 ◊  Q
                 ♣  A K 9 5
♠  --                              ♠  --
♡  --                              ♡  --
◊  6                               ◊  K J 7
♣  J 8 4 3                         ♣  10 6
                 ♠  --
                 ♡  --
                 ◊  A 10
                 ♣  Q 7 2
```

The obvious move is to return the king of diamonds
to pin dummy's queen, but East recognised the danger
that South might be able to pick up the club suit with a
third-round finesse. He therefore tried the cunning return of the jack of diamonds. South gave no thought to
running this to the queen (who in his right mind leads
jack from king-jack towards a bare queen in
dummy?), but went up with the ace and tested clubs
with the king and queen. When West followed with the
eight on the third round, declarer 'knew' that his last
card had to be the diamond king. So he went up with
the ace expecting the jack to fall. Tough!

Finally, here is a hand on which a defender with a
near-yarborough found a way of defeating a cast-iron
game.

```
               ♠ Q 5
               ♡ A K J
               ◇ K 10 9 4
               ♣ 8 7 5 3
♠ A K J 10 6 2                      ♠ 8 3
♡ Q 8 5 4                           ♡ 9 7 2
◇ 6                                 ◇ 7 5 3 2
♣ J 6                               ♣ 10 9 4 2
               ♠ 9 7 4
               ♡ 10 6 3
               ◇ A Q J 8
               ♣ A K Q
```

Both vulnerable.
Dealer South.

South	West	North	East
1NT	2♠	3♣	Pass
4◇	Pass	5◇	Pass
Pass	Pass		

West cashed his top spades and continued with the
jack of spades, which was ruffed in dummy with the
nine of diamonds. How did East defeat the contract?

Against an average declarer there is no chance, for
the heart finesse will inevitably yield the eleventh
trick. But South was an expert and East knew what he
was doing when he under-ruffed at trick three.

South shot up in his chair and took notice. What
possible reason could East have for this strange play?
The only explanation that seemed to make sense was
that he held three hearts headed by the queen along
with four clubs and four trumps. In that case he was
squeezed at trick three and a trump was the only card
he could spare.

South therefore cast around for an alternative to the
heart finesse, and he found one when his eye fell on

the ten of hearts. A criss-cross squeeze--what fun! He drew three rounds of trumps, cashed the king of hearts and the king and queen of clubs to confirm his view of the distribution, then led his last trump in the position shown below.

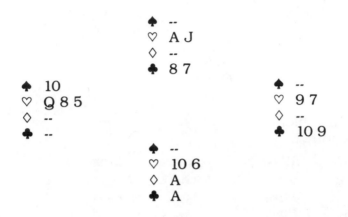

On the ace of diamonds West discarded the five of hearts and the heart jack was thrown from dummy. When East also threw a heart South crossed to the heart ace, confidently expecting the queen to fall. His faith in his own card-reading was shattered when East produced the nine, and he wondered why he continued to play in such a tricky game.

♠ ♡ ◇ ♣ ♠ ♡ ◇ ♣

Andersen THE LEBENSOHL CONVENTION COMPLETE .... $ 6.95
Baron THE BRIDGE PLAYER'S DICTIONARY $19.95
Bergen BETTER BIDDING WITH BERGEN,
      Vol. I, Uncontested Auctions $11.95
Bergen BETTER BIDDING WITH BERGEN,
      Vol. II, Competitive Auctions .... $ 9.95
Blackwood COMPLETE BOOK OF OPENING LEADS $14.95
Blackwood-Hanson PLAY FUNDAMENTALS .... $ 6.95
Boeder THINKING ABOUT IMPS $12.95
Bruno-Hardy 2 OVER 1 GAME FORCE: AN INTRODUCTION .... $ 9.95
Cole FISHHEADS .... $ 7.95
DeSerpa THE MEXICAN CONTRACT .... $ 5.95
Eber & Freeman HAVE I GOT A STORY FOR YOU .... $ 7.95
Feldheim FIVE CARD MAJOR BIDDING IN
      CONTRACT BRIDGE $11.95
Flannery THE FLANNERY 2 DIAMOND OPENING .... $ 7.95
Goldman ACES SCIENTIFIC .... $ 9.95
Goldman WINNERS AND LOSERS AT THE
      BRIDGE TABLE .... $ 3.95
Goodwin LET'S PLAY CARDS .... $ 9.95
Groner DUPLICATE BRIDGE DIRECTION $11.95
Hardy
      SPLINTERS AND OTHER SHORTNESS BIDS .... $ 7.95
      TWO-OVER-ONE GAME FORCE $14.95
      TWO-OVER-ONE GAME FORCE QUIZ BOOK $11.95
Harris BRIDGE DIRECTOR'S COMPANION (2nd Edition) $14.95
Karpin THE DRAWING OF TRUMPS — AND
      ITS POSTPONEMENT .... $ 9.95
Kay COMPLETE BOOK OF DUPLICATE BRIDGE $14.95
Kearse BRIDGE CONVENTIONS COMPLETE $24.95
Kelsey COUNTDOWN TO BETTER BRIDGE .... $ 9.95
Lampert THE FUN WAY TO ADVANCED BRIDGE .... $ 8.95
Lawrence
      CARD COMBINATIONS $11.95
      COMPLETE BOOK ON BALANCING $11.95
      COMPLETE BOOK ON OVERCALLS $11.95
      DYNAMIC DEFENSE $11.95
      FALSECARDS .... $ 9.95
      HAND EVALUATION $11.95
      HOW TO READ YOUR OPPONENTS' CARDS .... $ 9.95
      JUDGMENT AT BRIDGE .... $ 9.95
      PARTNERSHIP UNDERSTANDINGS .... $ 4.95
      PLAY BRIDGE WITH MIKE LAWRENCE $11.95

Lawrence
PLAY SWISS TEAMS WITH MIKE LAWRENCE .... $ 7.95
WORKBOOK ON THE TWO OVER ONE SYSTEM $11.95
Lawrence & Hanson WINNING BRIDGE INTANGIBLES .... $ 4.95
Lipkin INVITATION TO ANNIHILATION .... $ 8.95
Machlin TOURNAMENT BRIDGE: AN UNCENSORED MEMOIR .... $ 5.95
Michaels & Cohen 4-3-2-1 MANUAL .... $ 2.95
Penick BEGINNING BRIDGE COMPLETE .... $ 8.95
Penick BEGINNING BRIDGE QUIZZES .... $ 6.95
Powell TICKETS TO THE DEVIL .... $ 5.95
Reese & Hoffman PLAY IT AGAIN, SAM .... $ 7.95
Rosenkranz
BRIDGE: THE BIDDER'S GAME $12.95
TIPS FOR TOPS .... $ 9.95
MORE TIPS FOR TOPS .... $ 9.95
TRUMP LEADS .... $ 7.95
Rosenkranz & Alder BID TO WIN, PLAY FOR PLEASURE $11.95
Rosenkranz & Truscott BIDDING ON TARGET $10.95
Silverman
ELEMENTARY BRIDGE FIVE CARD MAJOR STUDENT TEXT ...... $ 2.75
INTERMEDIATE BRIDGE FIVE CARD MAJOR STUDENT TEXT .... $ 2.95
ADVANCED & DUPLICATE BRIDGE STUDENT TEXT .... $ 2.95
PLAY OF THE HAND AS DECLARER
& DEFENDER STUDENT TEXT .... $ 2.95
Simon
WHY YOU LOSE AT BRIDGE .... $ 9.95
Sontag & Steinberg IMPROVE YOUR BRIDGE — FAST .... $ 4.95
Stern EXPERT BRIDGE .... $ 6.95
Stewart & Baron
THE BRIDGE BOOK, Vol. 1, Beginning .... $ 9.95
THE BRIDGE BOOK, Vol. 2, Intermediate .... $ 9.95
THE BRIDGE BOOK, Vol. 3, Advanced .... $ 9.95
THE BRIDGE BOOK, Vol. 4, Defense .... $ 7.95
Von Elsner
THE ACE OF SPIES .... $ 5.95
CRUISE BRIDGE .... $ 5.95
EVERYTHING JAKE WITH ME .... $ 5.95
THE BEST OF JAKE WINKMAN .... $ 5.95
THE JAKE OF HEARTS .... $ 5.95
THE JAKE OF DIAMONDS .... $ 5.95
Woolsey
MATCHPOINTS $11.95
MODERN DEFENSIVE SIGNALLING .... $ 4.95
PARTNERSHIP DEFENSE .... $ 9.95